THE UNION WORKHOUSE

A Study Guide for Teachers and Local Historians

Learning Local History 3
General Editor: Alan Crosby

THE UNION WORKHOUSE
A Study Guide for Teachers and Local Historians

Andy Reid

Published by PHILLIMORE for
BRITISH ASSOCIATION FOR LOCAL HISTORY
with the aid of a grant from the
Calouste Gulbenkian Foundation

1994

Published for
BRITISH ASSOCIATION FOR LOCAL HISTORY

by
PHILLIMORE & CO. LTD.,
Shopwyke Manor Barn, Chichester, West Sussex

ISBN 0 85033 914 6

Printed and bound in Great Britain by
HARTNOLLS LTD.
Bodmin, Cornwall

Contents

List of Illustrations and Documents

Acknowledgements

Acknowledgement is made of the following for permission to reproduce source material: Norfolk Record Office; Norfolk Museums Service (Gressenhall Museum); Norfolk County Council; Norfolk Archaeological Unit; Derek A Edwards. Crown Copyright material in the Public Record Office is reproduced with the permission of the Controller of Her Majesty's Stationery Office. The ownership and origin of the source material is given in the caption for each item. The author expresses thanks for their assistance to Bridget Yates, the curator at the Norfolk Rural Life Museum, Gressenhall and to her colleagues; and to the staffs of the Public Record Office, Norfolk Record Office, Cambridge University Library, and Norwich Local Studies Library. Some of the ideas set out in the 'Investigations' section were developed by the author in collaboration with the staff of several schools which used visits to Gressenhall Workhouse, Norfolk as the basis for G.C.S.E. history assignments. The willingness of both staff and pupils to share and discuss their experience is gratefully acknowledged. Thanks are also due to David Dymond and Clive Paine, who offered useful guidance at the early stages of the writing of this book, and to Alan Crosby, who has been a most helpful and supportive editor.

This publication has been supported by a generous grant from the CALOUSTE GULBENKIAN FOUNDATION, to which the British Association for Local History expresses its warm thanks.

Editor's Foreword

The union workhouse has become a powerful symbol in the folk memory of poverty and deprivation—often detested, usually feared, almost always regarded with shame. Many of these institutions, which were mainly the product of the 1834 Poor Law Amendment Act, are still with us, revealed by their characteristic architecture and plan. And many of the principles which lay behind their construction, and which were the framework of the system within which they functioned, are detectable to this day.

In this superbly-researched book, Andy Reid shows how the history of a union workhouse can be reconstructed from the surviving physical evidence and a great range of printed and documentary sources. He demonstrates how the buildings and their occupants can be researched as part of local history in the National Curriculum—but the procedures which he explains, and the splendid range of sources which he uses as illustrations, will be of great relevance and interest to every local historian.

The British Association for Local History would like to express its collective thanks to Andy Reid for the painstaking preparation and writing of this book, undertaken despite many other calls on his time.

ALAN CROSBY
General Editor, B.A.L.H.

Author's Foreword

This publication has been produced with the needs of teachers of history in secondary schools in the era of the National Curriculum largely in mind. It may, however, prove of use to teachers at other levels—in primary schools, and in further education and adult education—and to others, such as local historians, with an interest in investigating the history of the union workhouse for themselves.

Its main purposes are:

* to provide a brief history of the union workhouse
* to describe the sources available for the investigation of an individual union workhouse
* to indicate where the sources are located and how access to them can be gained
* to discuss the nature and origins of the sources
* to suggest some themes for investigation by students

Most of the sources included relate to a single union workhouse, Gressenhall Workhouse in Norfolk. They are, however, of types which can be discovered for most other workhouses in England and Wales. The same applies to the suggested themes for investigation; Gressenhall Workhouse has been taken as the example, but the ideas can be applied to any union workhouse.

I
INTRODUCTION

Rationale

By whatever name it was known (the bastille, the spike, the union, or simply 'the house') the union workhouse epitomised the harsher realities of life in Victorian England and Wales. Some former workhouse buildings survive to this day, but many do not—it was not always easy to find alternative uses for them when they were no longer required for their original purposes. But the problem which they were designed to address—the problem of poverty—remains. Where responsibility for it lies, and how society should respond, continue to be matters for urgent debate. Thus the relevance of this subject matter for students can hardly be in doubt. Through investigation of the union workhouse they will develop an understanding of attitudes and responses to poverty in a past society, and this will enable them to bring new insights and perspectives to their understanding of poverty in the contemporary world. Investigations will also reveal that the union workhouse was not an unchanging feature of Victorian society, but one which evolved and developed as a result of national and local factors. It may also become apparent that the image which many people have of the workhouse (based to some extent on its portrayal by Dickens in *Oliver Twist*), though it contains elements of truth, is an over-simple and in some respects misleading one.

The process of investigation will also bring students into contact with a rich variety of historical sources. These include not only the workhouse buildings themselves, but also the huge archives which were generated by those responsible for the administration of the poor law at the national and local levels. Through the analysis and use of these sources, it will be possible to reconstruct the history of the workhouse as a site and as an institution, and to recreate the experience of the men, women and children whose lives were affected by it.

The National Curriculum framework for history provides opportunities at each stage, in both primary and secondary schools, for the investigation of a union workhouse. But whether it takes place within the National Curriculum or beyond it, such a study will prove immensely worthwhile, because it will both provide contact with historical content of intrinsic interest and importance, and offer outstanding opportunities to develop the skills of historical investigation and analysis. Go for it!

Historical Background

i) The origins of the union workhouse

The union workhouse came into existence as a result of the Poor Law Amendment Act of 1834. The 1834 Act was a radical piece of legislation. It swept away the 'Old Poor Law' which was inherited from the reign of Elizabeth I, and which had come under increasing pressure as a result of the economic and social changes of the late 18th and early 19th centuries. The Act established both a new administrative framework and a new approach to the relief of poverty. Before 1834, responsibility for the relief of the poor lay at the local level, with parish overseers of the poor (township overseers in the north of England) and county justices of the peace.

The Poor Law Amendment Act created a central body, the Poor Law Commission for England and Wales. The three commissioners were responsible for forming unions of parishes for the purposes of poor relief. The poor law unions were administered by boards of guardians elected by the open ballot of the ratepayers and property owners in each parish. There was a property qualification: guardians normally had to occupy property rated at £40 per year. Justices of the peace became ex-officio guardians. The activities of the boards of guardians were subject to the supervision of the Poor Law Commission; in practice, however, they retained considerable autonomy.

One of the first tasks of each board of guardians was to provide workhouse accommodation for the reception of those requiring poor relief. In some cases, it was possible to take over and adapt one or more of the workhouses which the union had inherited from a previous body. Before 1834 some groups of parishes had obtained private Acts of Parliament or had used the provisions of Gilbert's Act of 1782 to form themselves into larger groupings capable of supporting the expense of building and maintaining a large workhouse. These were, however, the minority; in most cases it was necessary for the new poor law union to build a workhouse from scratch.

In southern England, the formation of the unions and the building of workhouses took place in 1835-6, and proceeded relatively smoothly, with only sporadic resistance. However, when the commissioners turned their attention to northern England in 1837, there was much stronger opposition. In parts of the north it was not possible to build union workhouses until the 1850s or 1860s.

Those provisions of the Act of 1834 which related to the nature of the relief to be provided for the poor reflected, in diluted form, the recommendations of the *Poor Law Report* which had been published earlier in the same year. These had been greatly influenced by the Benthamite ideas of Edwin Chadwick and Nassau Senior. Their central principle was that the provision of poor relief should be concentrated in large workhouses. Conditions for the workhouse inmates should be 'less eligible' than those of the lowest-paid independent labourer, so that the workhouse would serve as a 'self acting test' of the applicant for relief. Only the destitute would wish to seek admission; the idle would be deterred. The harshness of the workhouse would, it was thought, act as a spur to the industry and enterprise of the able-bodied poor. The improvidence of the labouring classes would be replaced by self-reliance. Thus the moral climate of society in general would be reformed and—no less welcome—there would be a substantial reduction in the poor rates.

ii) Conditions in the union workhouse

The new punitive approach to poor relief inaugurated by the Act of 1834 was reflected in the organisation, diet, discipline and daily routine of the union workhouse. The inmates were subjected to the process of classification. They were divided into separate categories, each of which had its own segregated accommodation. This, notoriously, entailed the separation of husbands and wives, parents and children. The authors of the *Poor Law Report* had advocated a system of separate buildings for different classes of inmates, which would have spared the more vulnerable some of the rigours of 'less eligibility', but in practice it was the 'general mixed workhouse' which became the norm. Though they were confined in their separate quarters, all classes were accommodated on the same site and subjected, at least initially, to a similar regime.

The union workhouse was intended to be harsh, but the harshness was not intended to be uncontrolled. There were cases of abuse, of which the Andover scandal of 1846 was the most notorious, and no doubt there was also abuse which was never exposed. The union workhouse was, however, a highly regulated institution. The lives of the workhouse officers were in some ways as tightly constrained as those of the inmates, and this provided the latter with some protection and the possibility of redress against the worst excesses. Complaints by inmates were infrequent and were seldom vindicated by the authorities, but they could not be ignored.

Moreover, in many workhouses the officers and guardians did sometimes display compassion and kindness in their treatment of at least some groups of inmates— particularly the old, the sick and children. The education of those children in the workhouse was often taken rather more seriously than that of most of their contemporaries outside it. Expressions of appreciation and gratitude by former inmates were not unknown. For most inmates, the diet and physical conditions were in reality better than if the principle of 'less eligibility' had been enforced stringently. It was the carefully calculated monotony, the rigid routines and discipline, and the more subtle deprivations and degradations which were the most repressive features of the workhouse. Workhouse inmates lost their dignity; like the inmates of prisons and lunatic asylums, they also lost (if they had ever possessed it) the right to vote, a right which was not restored to them until 1918.

iii) Changes: 1834-1914

Between 1834 and 1914 there were gradual changes in the nature of the union workhouse as an institution. Firstly, the composition of the workhouse population altered. The provision of outdoor relief (the payment of money, or the provision of goods or services) to able-bodied adults meant that they constituted a smaller proportion of the workhouse population from the mid-19th century onwards. Initially, the intention had been that all outdoor relief to the able-bodied should cease, except for those requiring temporary relief for medical reasons: for the others the 'workhouse test' should be applied. But this proved to be impractical in northern England, where there was strong opposition to the building of workhouses and where outdoor relief continued to be given. In the south, too, the practice of giving outdoor relief to the able-bodied, by various means, gradually returned. After 1850 the inmates of workhouses were, in the main, the old, the sick, the handicapped, children and unmarried mothers. There was also a shifting population of vagrants or 'casuals', who were as far as possible kept completely separated from the other inmates.The conditions in which the inmates lived also changed, with increasing differentiation between the treatment given to different groups. For the vagrants, who had to endure the drudgery of oakum-picking or stone-breaking in exchange for a bowl of gruel and a night in an unheated casual ward, the workhouse remained harsh and inhospitable. The unmarried mothers, or 'unchaste women', were also isolated from the other inmates as far as possible. They were often excluded from the small privileges extended to others, because their poverty was deemed to result from their moral failings. There was a slight relaxation in the regime for the old, and greater concern was shown for the conditions of the handicapped. Towards the end of the century, it became an increasingly common (though not universal) practice for children to be removed from the workhouse altogether and placed in foster homes or in separate children's homes.

It was perhaps in the treatment of the sick that the most significant improvement took place. The development of the medical and nursing professions meant that expectations and standards were rising. Conditions in workhouse sick wards attracted increasing criticism, most notably from the medical journal, *The Lancet*, which in the 1860s exposed the appalling state of the workhouse infirmaries in London and campaigned for improvements. In some unions, sick wards were amalgamated and reorganised, while in others entirely new infirmaries were built. By 1900, there were strong forces for change in the administration of workhouses and in the poor law as a whole. The work of charitable individuals and organisations such as the Workhouse Visiting Society had for some time been creating a greater public awareness of workhouse conditions. They pressed strongly for improvements, especially in the treatment of the more vulnerable groups of inmates. By the end of the century there was also a different attitude to the causes of poverty; the work of Charles Booth and others had brought a recognition that unemployment should not necessarily be regarded as a consequence of the moral shortcomings of the unemployed.

A further factor was the extension of the franchise. At the national level this facilitated the election of MPs drawn from or sympathetic to the working class; at the local level it caused a change in the composition of boards of guardians. The franchise for the election of boards of guardians was made the same as that for parliamentary elections in 1894, and at the same time the property qualification, which had been reduced to £5 per year in 1892, was abolished. Working-class guardians could now be elected; women guardians, too, be-came more numerous. The reporting of their meetings in the local press, which had a rapidly growing readership, also helped to make the guardians more accountable to a wider public.

In 1905, the government set up a Royal Commission on the Poor Law and the Unemployed. Its members were unable to agree recommendations, and so in 1909 two reports appeared. The majority report favoured the thorough reform of the existing system; the minority report, whose signatories included George Lansbury (a future leader of the Parliamentary Labour Party) and Beatrice Webb, recommended the complete abolition of the poor law. No immediate action was taken on either report, but the introduction of old age pensions in 1908 and the first state sickness and unemployment insurance schemes in 1911 provided the basis for an alternative approach to social welfare. In 1913 it was decreed that union workhouses should thenceforward be referred to as 'poor law institutions'; nominally, the union workhouse had now ceased to exist.

iv) After 1914

Before the First World War the board of guardians of Poplar Union in the East End of London (of which George Lansbury had been a member from 1892) had begun to provide outdoor relief to the able-bodied unemployed, according to need and on a generous scale. With the onset of mass unemployment in 1921, the demands on the poor law authorities increased rapidly and several unions embraced 'Poplarism'. The government recognised the pressures on guardians to the extent of allowing them to borrow funds to meet their current expenses. The Poplar guardians, however, were jailed because they failed to make their contribution to the common fund for the relief of the poor in London as a whole. In 1926 Neville Chamberlain, minister of health in the Conservative government, secured the passage of the Board of Guardians (Default) Act. This allowed him to assume direct control of the administration of poor relief in unions where it was considered that the guardians were defaulting on their duties by distributing outdoor relief too liberally. It also had the effect of enabling the government to restrict the provision of relief to the families of striking coal miners.

The administrative structure of the Victorian poor law was finally dismantled by the Local Government Act of 1929, which took effect on 31 March 1930. The boards of guardians were dissolved and their responsibilities were transferred to the county and county borough councils. The poor law institutions were now known as 'public assistance institutions'. Some were converted for more specialised purposes, but most remained in use, with essentially the same functions and the same groups of inmates, until after the Second World War. The last Poor Law (Amendment) Act was passed in 1938; one of its provisions was that old people in poor law institutions should receive pocket money of 2s. per week.

The poor law was finally brought to an end by the National Assistance Act of 1948, one of the measures which inaugurated the welfare state. Since then, many workhouse buildings have been demolished. Some have been allowed to fall into dereliction. Others have been converted to serve other purposes, most commonly as hospitals or old people's homes, though other uses—for example as a school or a hotel—are known.

Gressenhall Workhouse

Most of the sources included in this book relate to one workhouse: the workhouse of the Mitford and Launditch Union at Gressenhall in Norfolk. Occasional use is made of sources relating to two other Norfolk workhouses—the Depwade Union Workhouse at Pulham St Mary Magdalen and the Loddon and Clavering Union Workhouse at Heckingham. However, almost all the sources are of a kind which can be found for workhouses all over England and Wales.

In one respect, Gressenhall Workhouse (though far from unique in East Anglia) is untypical of the majority of workhouses in the country as a whole: its main buildings date from before 1834. They were erected in 1776-7 to serve as the 'house of industry' for the parishes in the hundreds (districts) of Mitford and Launditch. The property owners of these parishes, like those in several other parts of East Anglia, had obtained a private Act of Parliament allowing them to form an incorporation for the purposes of poor relief. This enabled them to raise a large enough sum on the security of the poor rates to fund the building of a house of industry in which the poor could be accommodated and set to work. The total cost of the buildings and the 63-acre estate which surrounded them was £15,000, and the house of industry was erected on a scale and in a style which betokened a more generous attitude to the relief of the poor than was to obtain after 1834. In 1836, following the passage of the Poor Law Amendment Act two years earlier, the Mitford and Launditch Incorporation was dissolved and superseded by the Mitford and Launditch Union. The workhouse was altered and extended, to permit the classification and the stricter disciplinary regime which were required under the new poor law. £4,800 was borrowed to pay for the necessary alterations and additions. The work was not done efficiently (the clerk of the works was alleged to have been a habitual drunkard) but the appearance of the workhouse was transformed. Four policemen stood by when the inmates were classified and placed in their new separate quarters in the autumn of 1836, but there was no trouble.

After 1836, life at Gressenhall was similar to that at any other workhouse. The subsequent changes in the fabric and organisation of the buildings were likewise similar to those which were made at many other workhouses at about the same time. In 1853, a slight softening of attitudes was indicated by the building of a separate ward for 'respectable' elderly married couples. A chapel was built with funds raised by private subscription in 1868. In 1870-1, at a cost of nearly £1,800, the guardians converted one wing of the main building into the workhouse infirmary and erected a separate fever ward and other new buildings. There was a final phase of new building at the turn of the century, when a loan of £3,650 was obtained to finance the improvement of the infirmary and kitchens, the installation of main drainage and a hot water supply and the construction of a steam laundry.

After 1930, many of the walls which divided the site into separate exercise yards were demolished, lawns were laid out and shrubs were planted. The main building became an old people's home after 1948, with the former casual wards providing emergency housing for homeless families. In 1975, the entire site was transferred to the Norfolk Museums

Service. Part of the main building now houses the Norfolk Archaeological Unit, and the remainder of the site is occupied by the Norfolk Rural Life Museum. The museum has a small display on the history of the workhouse, linked to one of the former punishment cells which has been opened to the public. The workhouse buildings may be explored by arrangement with the Museum Education Officer (tel. 0362 860294).

1. *Gressenhall Workhouse, Mitford and Launditch Union* (Andy Reid)

2. *Gressenhall Workhouse* (Norfolk Archaeological Unit: Derek A. Edwards) The large central H-shaped block, and the eastern and south-eastern wings which form an L-shaped extension to the right in the photograph, were built in 1776-7. The symmetry of the 18th-century design would have been completed by western and south-western wings, which were planned but never built. The boundary wall and most of the buildings along the western edge of the site date from 1836-7. The chapel was erected by public subscription in 1868: before then religious services were held in the dining hall in the main block. Immediately south of it is the small building erected in 1853 to provide accommodation for elderly married couples. The building adjoining the southern boundary wall, east of the main gate, was built in 1871 as a fever ward. The long low structure at the north-eastern corner of the site was erected in the period 1895-1902 as a steam laundry. The courtyard on the northern side of the central H-shaped block has recently been roofed over to provide display space for the Norfolk Rural Life Museum.

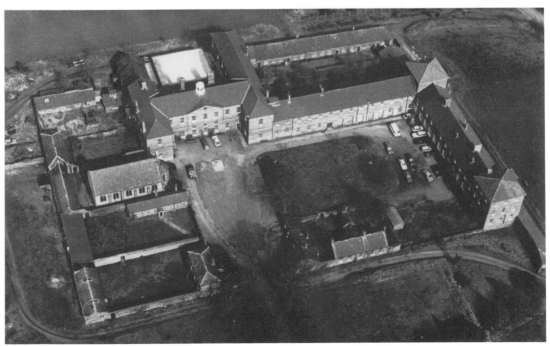

3. *South elevation of the east wing, Gressenhall Workhouse* (Norfolk Museums Service: Andy Reid) This part of the building was erected in 1776-7 and originally boasted an open arcade, described sarcastically in 1836 by Dr James Kay, the assistant poor law commissioner, as 'not unlike the streets of Bologna'. The arcade is clearly visible in a painting of 1810 (Source 18). Before 1836, the eastern and south-eastern wings had been divided into single rooms or 'cottages' for families. Extensive and costly modifications were necessary to create the segregated accommodation required under the new poor law. The arcade, which also extended along the western side of the south-eastern wing, was blocked up in stages, partly in 1836 and partly later in the 19th century and in the period 1895-1902.

4. *The south east wing, Gressenhall Workhouse* (Andy Reid) In 1871 this wing was modified to serve as the workhouse infirmary, and two two-storey lean-to extensions containing toilets were built. The one nearer to the camera was further extended in the late 1890s. Source 19 provides a similar view dating from the turn of the century.

II
LOCATING AND USING SOURCES

Workhouse Buildings

A quick way to discover the locations of former workhouses is to consult 19th or early 20th-century county trade directories, which should give details of all the poor law unions and their respective workhouses. Having established from this source the parish in which the workhouse lay, the precise location can be established from early Ordnance Survey maps, copies of which are available in most local history libraries. Many rural workhouses were erected in isolated positions: few people, it seems, wanted to have a workhouse on their doorstep. Many workhouse buildings no longer exist, but if they survive they are seldom difficult to identify on the ground.

The next step will be to negotiate access to the site. This is not always straightforward. If the buildings are still intact and are still used for institutional purposes, those responsible for them will need to be reassured that the interests of the patients or residents will be protected. Their needs may dictate that limits are imposed on the extent to which the buildings can be explored. If the buildings are derelict, exploring them may involve an unacceptable element of risk. It would be rash to assume that access to the site of a workhouse will be automatic and without problems. Nevertheless, if it can be achieved, a visit can prove very worthwhile.

Although workhouse buildings, with their unmistakably institutional character, are easy to recognise, they do not all conform to the same plan, and the variations between them can be interesting and instructive. The majority of large workhouses date from the years immediately after the passing of the Poor Law Amendment Act of 1834. The poor law commissioners issued model workhouse plans drawn up by the previously unknown architect Sampson Kempthorne, but poor law unions were not obliged to follow them. In practice the plan decided upon would depend on negotiation between the board of guardians of the union concerned and its chosen architect, against the background of local conditions. An ambitious architect might be able to persuade a board to build a grander workhouse than it had originally contemplated.

Some large workhouses were erected before 1834 for other bodies—boroughs, or 'incorporations' or unions of parishes formed under the provisions of earlier acts of parliament. In northern England, because of the strong initial opposition to the new poor law, many unions did not build large workhouses until the 1850s or 1860s. In some cases boards of guardians discovered that their original arrangements for workhouse accommodation had not been adequate, and so built a new workhouse at a later stage.

All workhouses underwent major or minor modifications at various points in the 19th and 20th centuries in response to changing patterns of use and changing conceptions of what was required.

Each group of workhouse buildings therefore has an individual history, a history which will be reflected in the surviving physical evidence on the site. Through investigation of the evidence it should be possible to reconstruct elements of the history of the workhouse and to make deductions about the uses to which different parts of the site were put. It will also be possible to gain insights into the conditions of life for inmates and officers.

Manuscript and Printed Sources

i) Records of the poor law unions

The administration of the affairs of a poor law union and its workhouse was the responsibility of an elected board of guardians. The board was required to keep minutes of its own meetings, and a range of other records were also kept. In 1930, when the boards of guardians ceased to exist, their records were normally transferred to the county and county borough councils which had taken over the boards' responsibilities. Today these records are usually to be found in the local record office. The completeness of holdings varies considerably, however, and it cannot be guaranteed that the records of a specific union will be found in quantity in the record office. If they are not there enquiries could be made of other branches of the county or metropolitan borough council, or of the local hospital authorities. In cases where the former workhouse buildings are still used for institutional purposes, an approach to the institution itself may be worthwhile. It may sometimes be the case that while most of the records are in the record office, others 'strayed' before the collection was deposited there and may turn up in other places.

A guide to poor law union records, in four parts, has been published recently (1993) by J.S.W. Gibson (Harts Cottage, Church Hanborough, Oxfordshire, OX8 8AB). This lists all known local holdings and includes reference to some of the sources in the Public Record Office which are discussed in the next section (see also the *bibliography* at the end of this book).

The *minute books* of the board of guardians are an important source of evidence about the union workhouse, both as a site and as an institution. They were compiled in accordance with a formula prescribed by the national poor law authorities and so do not vary greatly in appearance from union to union. In some, but not all, cases the minutes are indexed, which speeds up the process of following particular themes. The guardians met weekly or fortnightly, and always had a great deal of routine business to transact, much of it extremely tedious.

It is easy to be put off by the sheer volume of the minute books, but patience can be rewarded. Among the interminable administrative and financial minutiae can be found some very useful material. If the union being investigated is one of the majority in which a new workhouse was built in the 1830s or afterwards, there will be references to negotiations with the architect and the construction of the buildings. There will also be mention throughout the 19th and early 20th centuries of large and small alterations and other works on the buildings. Some of these references may shed light on the physical evidence which can be seen on the site today. There may also be material relating to the functions of different parts of the site and buildings at different times.

Use of the minute books can also help the investigator to 'populate' the buildings. There will be references to the appointment, payment, and resignation or dismissal of workhouse officers, and to incidents which involved them. Changes in the numbers of inmates from week to week, and the names of some if not all of those admitted and discharged, may be recorded. There will also be much anecdotal material on named individual inmates, particularly those who stood out because they came into conflict with the workhouse authorities. Evidence on various aspects of life in the workhouse will be found, but this will be in the form of occasional references, and must be worked for! Charitable donations to the workhouse may be recorded, and visitors noted. A notable visitor to Gressenhall Workhouse in 1860 was Prince Napoleon of France, who stayed for several hours and expressed himself 'much pleased and satisfied with the extreme cleanliness and general appearance of the House'.

It is worth emphasising that the picture of workhouse life provided by the minute books is far from being a complete one. It was change or controversy, the unusual or the untoward, which tended to occasion entries. That which was taken for granted and continued unchanged, or was not significant enough to attract attention, goes unrecorded. Aspects of the inmates' lives about which it would be interesting to know more (the clothes they wore, for example) may be mentioned but seldom. Since it was only the decisions which were recorded, the minutes do not even give a very full picture of what happened at the guardians' meetings. If the press was admitted, the reports in the local papers immediately make clear how much is concealed by the clipped, parsimonious entries in the minute books.

In addition to the minutes of the meetings of the full board of guardians, it may also be possible to consult minute books kept by committees established by the guardians to supervise particular aspects of workhouse administration. The minutes of the *visiting committee* (which in the late 19th century tended to be replaced by a *house committee*) will yield more interesting detail about life in the workhouse than those of, for example, the *finance committee*. Among the other records of poor law unions are ledgers which record the guardians' financial transactions (about which there is also much information in the minute books) and, for some unions, *registers of admissions and discharges* of inmates.

There may also be *plans of the workhouse*, drawn up in connection with the original building operations or subsequent alterations. When they survive these will be an invaluable source for the interpretation of the site and buildings; unfortunately, in many cases (including Mitford and Launditch Union) they no longer exist, a situation which becomes even more frustrating when references in other sources make it apparent that they were once extant. One just has to be philosophical about this—and it is always possible that lost items may turn up eventually.

There may also be a variety of other interesting and useful sources among the records of a poor law union:

* a **workhouse master's journal** or report book, in which he kept a weekly record of events in the workhouse
* a **punishment book**, with lists of the inmates punished, their offences and the punishments given
* **printed dietaries**, setting out the weekly diet for different classes of inmate
* **correspondence**
* records kept by **the chaplain, the medical officer, and relieving officers** (who received applications for relief, distributed outdoor relief in appropriate cases, and issued orders for admission to the workhouse)
* **registers of births and deaths** in the workhouse
* **registers of creeds** of inmates
* records relating to the **consumption of alcohol and tobacco** by inmates
* records relating to **vagrants**
* other **miscellanea**

ii) Records of the national poor law authorities

The Poor Law Commission for England and Wales, created by the Poor Law Amendment Act of 1834, consisted of three commissioners, who appointed a number of assistant commissioners to represent them in different parts of the country and to provide a link between the central and local bodies. In 1847 the Commission was replaced by the Poor Law Board, and the post of assistant poor law commissioner was replaced by that of poor law inspector. The Poor Law Board took over and continued the series of records established by the Poor Law Commission. In 1871 the Poor Law Board was absorbed by the Local Government Board (the poor law inspectors becoming known as general inspectors), which in turn took over and continued the same series of records. In 1919 the Local Government Board was absorbed by the Ministry of Health and the accumulated records passed to the new body. They are now in the Public Record Office at Kew.

Kew may be a rather inconvenient place to get to, but it is well worth making the effort. The Public Record Office has a large free car park, and Kew Gardens station is nearby. Having completed the formality of obtaining a reader's ticket, one has access to a vast hoard of material illustrating the operation of the new poor law in every part of England and Wales. The relevant sources are in classes prefixed by the letters MH (standing for Ministry of Health, the body to which the material ultimately descended).

Class MH12 contains nearly 17,000 volumes of correspondence covering the period 1834-1900 (most of the correspondence for the period after 1900 having been destroyed by bombing during the Second World War), referred to collectively as the poor law union papers. The volumes are arranged under unions, with each volume containing about four years' correspondence. The participants were as follows:

* Boards of guardians
* Individual guardians
* Parish overseers and vestries
* Poor Law Commission (1834-1847)
* Poor Law Board (1847-1871)
* Local Government Board (1871-1900)
* Assistant poor law commissioners (to 1847)
* Poor law inspectors (from 1847)
* General inspectors (from 1871)
* Workhouse inmates (occasionally)
* Others

In many cases, copies of the replies sent by the central body are also preserved, together with memoranda and comments by assistant poor law commissioners, poor law inspectors and other officials. Much of the material sent in both directions is routine, consisting of printed forms with the relevant details written in, and so searching the volumes can be rather gruelling; but, as with the minute books of the poor law unions, patience can be rewarded. Now and then an item will turn up which, by vividly illuminating some aspect of the workhouse experience, makes the search worthwhile.

The material discovered in MH12 will tend to relate to the same themes as those touched upon by the minute books of the boards of guardians, but the evidence provided is often much more detailed and suggestive. There will undoubtedly be correspondence concerning building works, large and small, at the workhouse, including, occasionally, small plans or sketches. Material relating to the internal organisation of the buildings will also be found. There are questionnaires which were returned when a workhouse officer was appointed, providing details of the successful applicant's qualifications and personal circumstances, together with other material relating to the conduct of the workhouse officers. If, for example, an officer was sacked, or there was some doubt about his or her competence or integrity, the reasons would usually be explained to the central body in detail.

Statistical information about the workhouse inmates would often be sent in by the local authorities on the printed forms provided—the completed forms will be found in MH12. If the local board of guardians required guidance on how to handle the case of a particular individual, detailed biographical and anecdotal information about the person concerned might be supplied. It should be borne in mind, however, that it is the rebellious and recalcitrant about whom most will be discovered: those who bowed their heads and shut their mouths tend to go unnoticed. Still, it is from experience of those who kicked against the system that most can be learned about how the system worked and in this sense the recorded lives of the rebellious can shed much light on the unrecorded lives of the docile. Occasionally, there will be a letter of complaint from a workhouse inmate: all such complaints had to be investigated but in very few cases were they considered by the authorities to have any justification.

The volumes of correspondence also provide much general material on various aspects of workhouse life. The assistant poor law commissioners contributed their share of it, and from 1847 the poor law inspectors sent in a report on a printed form after every visit to a workhouse. On this they were able to draw attention to any features of the management which they considered unsatisfactory. Reports on the workhouse school, and reports from visiting commissioners in lunacy, may also turn up from time to time in the correspondence.

Class MH32, *assistant commissioners' and inspectors' correspondence*, contains bound volumes of correspondence and other material of a more general nature (often involving more than one poor law union) between the assistant commissioners and inspectors and the central body.

Poor law union plans are collected in class MH14. The plans all date from the period 1861-1900, and were originally included in the volumes of correspondence in class MH12. They are not as numerous as one might hope: many unions are not represented in the collection at all.

Workhouse expenditure is summarised, union by union, in large ledgers in class MH34. The expenditure referred to is that on the site and buildings which was sufficiently major to necessitate the borrowing of money by the board of guardians. This source enables the dates of major works in the period 1834-1901 to be established rapidly.

Other sources in the Public Record Office relevant to the investigation of a union workhouse include *registers of workhouse officers* for the period 1837-1921 (MH9), *circulars* sent out by the central authorities, 1834-1919 (MH10), *diaries of visiting officers* of metropolitan casual wards (MH18) and some further files of *correspondence* mainly for the period 1901-1919 (MH48).

iii) Other manuscript and printed sources

Maps of various kinds and dates will provide evidence for the physical layout of the workhouse. These will be invaluable if there are no surviving detailed plans, and useful even if there are. The scale of *Ordnance Survey 1:2500 maps* ('25-inch' maps) is large enough to show small structures as well as large, and even internal dividing walls (many of which may now have disappeared) are depicted with some clarity. Comparisons of different editions will reveal major changes which took place between their respective dates of publication. For workhouses in large towns, an even more useful source will be the *Ordnance Survey 1:500 town plans*, published simultaneously with the first edition of the 1:2500 maps. The dates of survey and publication vary across the country.

In urban areas, too, workhouses are often shown on *town plans* produced by private enterprise in the period before the publication of the Ordnance Survey 1:500 plans. Copies of the 1:2500 maps and other plans may be available for consultation and copying in local reference libraries and record offices. OS maps more than 50 years old are out of copyright.

If local libraries do not hold copies, one place where the maps will certainly be found is the map library of the British Library in London.

A possible earlier source for the outline plan of workhouses in rural areas in the late 1830s or 1840s is the *tithe map* for the parish in which the workhouse was situated. If workhouse buildings already existed at the time of parliamentary enclosure, the *enclosure map* may show them. Parliamentary enclosure did not happen everywhere, and it took place at different dates in different places. In most places, however, it was completed before 1834. Both tithe and enclosure maps need to be used with caution. In neither case was accurate portrayal of buildings important to the purpose of the map, and (in the case of enclosure maps) the scale used was often too small to encourage confidence that it was achieved. However, these two sources are certainly well worth consulting.

The names and personal details of the workhouse officers and the details, if not always the names, of the inmates can be found in the *census enumerator's books* for 1841, 1851, 1861, 1871, 1881 and 1891. The nature of this source has already been described in another book in this series, *The Late Victorian Town*, by Frank Grace. The books which were used in workhouses and other institutions are slightly different from the standard ones, but their content is substantially the same.

The books for the 1841 census provide the following information:
* the names of the officers
* the names or initials of the inmates
* the occupations of the officers and those of the inmates who were regarded as having occupations
* the ages of all those listed (the ages of those over 15 being given as the nearest multiple of five below the actual age)
* for each person, whether he or she was born inside or outside the county in which the workhouse was situated

From the 1851 census onwards, the books include:
* the precise age of each person listed
* the actual place of birth of each person

The census enumerator for a workhouse would normally be the master, and he would sometimes preserve the anonymity of the inmates who, like prisoners in gaols, might be recorded by their initials rather than by their full names; but this did not always happen.

Census enumerators' books may be read on microfilm at the Public Record Office (in the basement of the Chancery Lane branch in central London at the time of writing). It may well not be necessary to travel to London, however, because the local record office and/ or local history library will hold copies of microfilms for the area which they serve. The information contained in the books is also gradually becoming available in the form of computer databases.

A quicker way to find the names of at least some of the workhouse officers is to consult *trade directories*, some of which may be available in the reference section of the local public library. These generally include entries for each poor law union, with details of the parishes included in the union; the date of the erection, cost and capacity of the workhouse; the actual number of inmates; and the annual expenditure of the union; and the names of the principal officers.

Local newspapers can provide much information about workhouse life. The reference library, local history library or record office may hold series of some of the relevant newspapers. If not, and if the newspaper is still in publication, it may be worth enquiring at its offices. Failing that, it will be necessary to make a visit to the Newspaper Division of the British Library at Colindale, North London. This is in any case well worth a visit. It is easy to get to, the building being very near to Colindale underground station; the formalities involved in securing admission are minimal; the holdings are immense and the arrangements for photocopying are very efficient. Wherever it is done, however, searching a newspaper can be time consuming. They are rarely indexed and, because they are such rich sources for so many subjects, it is easy to get distracted. It is probably best to start by following up leads obtained from other sources rather than to search randomly.

Four kinds of material in newspapers may be relevant:

* *Advertisements* Two kinds of advertisements are likely to be useful. Firstly, there are those for workhouse officers. These state the salary provided, and may also shed a little light on the conditions under which the person appointed would work. Secondly, there are advertisements soliciting tenders for the provision of goods or services to the workhouse by contractors. From these it is possible to gain insights into the food the inmates ate, the clothes they wore, and other details of their lives. Where the advertisement seeks tenders for building work, there may be some indication of the changes which the guardians wished to make in the buildings.
* *Letters* Letters to the local newspapers may draw attention to scandals and matters of controversy, and in the process shed light both on contemporary attitudes and on aspects of workhouse life.
* *News items* The newspaper may refer to events such as riots or fires in the workhouse. More prosaically, there may be newspaper reports which provide details of the Christmas dinner served to the suitably grateful workhouse inmates.
* *Reports of the meetings of boards of guardians* Many boards of guardians were slow to allow reporters from the local press to attend their weekly or fortnightly meetings, and when they eventually did so, it was no doubt with some hesitation and not a few misgivings on the part of some of their members. In the Mitford and Launditch Union it was the new board, elected after the extension of the franchise and the abolition of the property qualification for guardians in 1894, which at its first meeting on 5 January 1895 voted by 21-15 (with 13 abstentions) to admit the press.

For the first few years after this decision, reports of the board's meetings were often given considerable space in the local newspapers, and some of them make fascinating reading. The arguments, controversies and faction fights largely concealed by the bland entries in the minute books now become more fully visible, and it is possible to get a better feel of the proceedings when some of the dialogue is reported verbatim. The reporting could be selective, however, and where possible it would be desirable to analyse the coverage provided by two or more newspapers of different political persuasions in order to obtain an overall view.

A wide range of printed sources which are national rather than local in nature can provide both detailed local information and the wider national context within which to understand the local events. *Official publications* of various kinds provide an enormous quantity of material on virtually every aspect of the administration of the poor law. The *Poor Law Report* of 1834 sets out the thinking which resulted in the creation of the union workhouse, and includes evidence, much of it anecdotal and highly prejudicial, on the functioning of the workhouses which already existed before the passage of the Poor Law Amendment Act later in the same year. The *Annual Reports of the Poor Law Commissioners*, particularly for the years immediately after 1834, are invaluable. As well as general material, they also include detailed reports by assistant commissioners on developments in specific localities. The *Reports of the Select Committee on the Relief of the Poor* (1837-8), and the *Report of the Lords' Select Committee on the Operation of the Poor Law Amendment Act* (1837-8) provide rich veins of local material (in the former, Ampthill Union in Bedfordshire is particularly well represented), including the testimony of the poor themselves.

The *Report of the Select Committee on the Andover Union* (1846), and the minutes of evidence taken by the committee, enable the scandal at Andover workhouse, which contributed to the demise of the Poor Law Commission and its replacement by the Poor Law Board, to be studied in detail. The majority and minority *Reports of the Royal Commission on the Poor Law and the Unemployed* (1909) provide a mass of material on the administration of the poor law in the first decade of the 20th century.

Other parliamentary papers (often known as 'blue books') contain tabulated returns from poor law unions relating to matters as various as the numbers of illegitimate children born in workhouses, the dietaries used, and the arrangements made for the reception of the 'casual poor'. Some of the blue books also contain detailed case studies and minutes of evidence relating to specific institutions, the metropolitan workhouses being particularly thoroughly investigated.

The regulations and orders of the national poor law authorities, which defined the regime to be implemented in workhouses, are obviously an important source. They were reprinted in *Glen's Poor Law Orders*, a standard reference work for boards of guardians: new updated editions were produced at regular intervals.

Detailed local information set within a wider context can also be found in the volumes of *papers delivered to Poor Law Conferences*. These were gatherings of guardians and national officials which took place on a regional basis during the period 1875-1930. Other useful sources, for earlier periods, include the *Journal of the Workhouse Visiting Society*

(1859-1865), and, from a perspective hostile to the new poor law, *The Book of the Bastilles* edited by G.R. Wythen Baxter (1841).

The standard general historical works which were produced while the poor law was still in existence are *English Poor Law History* (three volumes, 1927-9) and *English Poor Law Policy* (1910) both by Sidney and Beatrice Webb, and Sir George Nicholls' two volume *History of the English Poor Law* with a third volume by Thomas Mackay covering the period up to the date of publication (1899). To these could be added the large number of other contemporary works dealing with particular aspects of workhouse life and administration. Lists of these will be found in the bibliographies of modern historical works such as those listed in the bibliography on pages 89-90. Two particularly readable modern studies of workhouse life are *The Workhouse* by Norman Longmate (1974) and *The Workhouse System 1834-1929* by M.A. Crowther (1981).

Contemporary fiction can convey a powerful impression of the atmosphere of a workhouse. Dickens wrote evocatively about workhouse conditions in *Oliver Twist*, and also in *Little Dorrit*. *Jessie Phillips, a Tale of the Present Day*, by Frances Trollope (1844) is set in a workhouse. Similarly vivid (and, arguably, more reliable) material may be found in autobiographical accounts such as those by George Lansbury (in *My Life*, 1928) and Charles Chaplin (*My Autobiography*, 1964). Among many other contemporary accounts of workhouse life which could be mentioned is that by H. Rider Haggard, who wrote vividly about conditions in the workhouse of the Loddon and Clavering Union at Heckingham in Norfolk in *A Farmer's Year* (1899).

Other Sources

It may be possible to find *photographs* of the workhouse, of its officers and even (though this is less likely) of its inmates. The reference library, local history library, record office or museums service will be the first points of enquiry here. In addition, there may be photographs in the possession of former officers of the institution or their descendants, and an appeal through the correspondence columns of the local newspaper may prove worthwhile. Information about any new sources discovered in this way should be lodged, with the permission of the owners, with the local archive, library or museum services.

Other *visual sources* may be available—it was not unknown for postcards or even Christmas cards showing workhouse buildings to be produced. There may also be paintings of the buildings. The *artefacts* associated with workhouses were generally not of great intrinsic value or of a kind likely to be sought after by later generations. But it is possible that some of the furniture, crockery or cutlery, particularly that used in the later periods of the institution's life, may survive. If they do, they may help to convey something of the atmosphere of the building in which they were used.

Contemporary music relating to workhouses is not plentiful, but there are some relevant folk songs. An example is 'The New Gruel Shops' (reprinted, with a score, in

R. Palmer [ed.] *A Touch on the Times* [1974]). The **oral testimony** of former inmates and others who remember the workhouse may be of great value. It will, of course, apply only to the period within living memory, when the original harshness of the system had been mitigated to some extent by the more humane attitudes which developed towards the end of the 19th century. Inevitably, new oral evidence will become less and less easy to obtain as the years pass, but it is to be hoped that much may be preserved on tape or in the form of transcripts.

Even if contact with those with first hand experience of the pre-1930 workhouse is possible, the recording of oral testimony may not be easy. For many people, association with the workhouse was a matter of shame, and there may be an understandable reluctance to recall and share experiences of workhouse life. Sensitivity and tact will be needed. Oral evidence, however, is exceptionally valuable in illuminating the nature of the system as it was experienced by those whose lives were lived in the shadow of the workhouse.

5. *Pulham Market Workhouse, Depwade Union* (Norfolk Archaeological Unit: Derek A. Edwards) Pulham Market Workhouse was built in 1836-7 to a symmetrical design consisting of a cross inside an octagon. The architect, William Thorold—described by Dr Kay as 'a cunning man'—persuaded the Depwade board of guardians to spend considerably more on their new workhouse than they had originally intended. The low outside wall provided a defence against the raids of the local poor while the buildings were being erected. Comparison with Source 6 reveals that some features of the 19th-century plan have subsequently disappeared. At the time when this photograph was taken the main buildings were being used as a hotel; this has now closed.

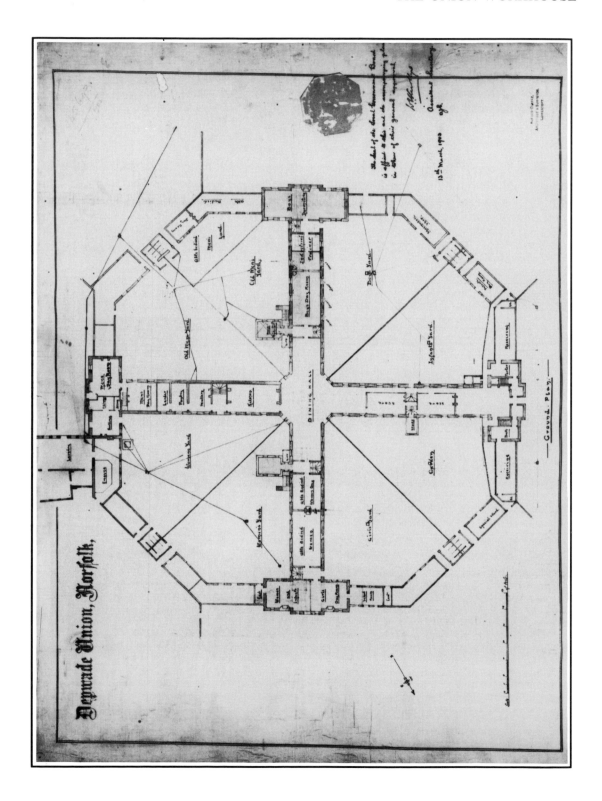

Elmham District,

Resolved upon the recommendation of the Visiting Committee that John Crow now a pauper of East Bercham be employed as Shoemaker at the Gressenhall Workhouse at the wages of seven shillings per week.

Honor the wife of James Dickerson an Inmate of the Workhouse was brought before the Board on complaint of the Master for throwing some Bread over into the Able bodied mens wards. Ordered that she be confined in the Dungeon to morrow for 8 Hours.

Benj: Francis.
Chairman Residing —

6. (Opposite) *Plan of Pulham Market Workhouse, Depwade Union, 1903* (Norfolk Record Office, C/GP3/213) This plan was made in connection with alterations and additions to the workhouse costing £1,254. The guardians sent it, with detailed written specifications, to the Local Government Board. When the proposals had been approved the plan and specification were returned to the guardians with the Board's seal attached. Many of the buildings shown in this plan survive: see Source 5.

7. (Above) *Punishment of Honor Dickerson* (minute book of the board of guardians of Mitford and Launditch Union, 1 February 1841: Norfolk Record Office, C/GP14/4) Honor Dickerson had presumably intended to give the bread to her husband. Despite this offence she seems later to have been regarded as an exemplary inmate. In 1844 she was given £1 'as a reward for good conduct and for her services as a laundry woman', and the following year she received a similar 'gratuitous remuneration'. In May 1845, the former master, Mr Pinson, took Honor Dickerson into his service at Norwich Castle; her children, however, remained at Gressenhall. In 1868, as an old woman, she returned to her place of birth in Mitford and Launditch, and to the pages of the guardians' minute book.

It appeared by a statement presented by the Master that during the last week 24 paupers were admitted into the workhouse 28 were discharged none died and 250 remain.

It appeared by the visitors' book that Sir John Walsham the Assistant Poor Law Commissioner had unexpectedly visited the workhouse on the 16th instant and reported that he had found the whole establishment in most excellent order and considered the recent alterations to be an admirable improvement.

Ordered that a ventilator be placed in the old men's lower room requiring 24 feet of perforated zinc piping at 9d per foot according to the plan recommended by Sir John Walsham.

Agreed that iron underground piping be laid down in the yards of the union workhouse according to the tender of the Messrs Hambling at a cost not exceeding 10.9.4 subject to a deduction to be made for the use of old materials.

Ordered that Benjamin High of Oxwick be taken before the magistrates upon the complaint of the Master of the workhouse charging him with having deserted his children.

Ordered that John Ringrose a person maintained in the union workhouse be taken before the magistrates for misbehaviour in the workhouse.Ordered that the Clerk do write to Sir John Walsham thanking him in the name of the Guardians for his recent present of bats and balls to the boys in the workhouse school.

8. *Extracts from the minutes of the meeting of the board of guardians of Mitford and Launditch Union, 22 June 1846* (Norfolk Record Office, C/GP14/7) This was a quarterly meeting, when bills were settled and salaries paid, and so there was more than the usual volume of financial business to deal with. With that qualification, however, the range of matters dealt with by the board of guardians is fairly typical.

1. *Date of last previous visit*: 26th February, 1865

2. *Is the workhouse generally adequate to the wants of the union, in respect of size and internal arrangment?* In respect of size this large old "Hundred House" is abundantly adequate, and its internal arrangements generally are not unsatisfactory. But in respect of several minor details the management (owing to its having been too much be-praised by Assistant Commissioners at first) has stood still for the last 30 years, and is now evidently behind-hand.

5. *Is the workhouse school well managed?* ... Yes—but Mr Bowyer [HMI] has not inspected these schools since the 27th September 1865. The Chaplain's reports are very satisfactory.

6. *What is the number of inmates not in communion with the Church of England, and what arrangements, if any, exist for affording them the consolation and instruction of ministers of their own separate persuasion?* There are 16 nominal Dissenters now in the workhouse, but they all conform to the services of the Church.

8. *Are there vagrant wards in the workhouse, and are they sufficient? Are the arrangements for setting the vagrants to work effective?* ... The men's refractory is used as the vagrant ward—female vagrants being placed in a small room opening into the dining hall and sometimes in the female refractory. These refractories are large for refractories, but they look like what they are. Vagrants however seldom travel along this line of country ...

17. *Has any marked change taken place in the state of the workhouse, the number of the inmates, or the general condition of the union, since your last visit?* The sanitary condition of the workhouse is very good, and so also, I believe, is that of the union generally. The number of workhouse inmates is rather lower than at this time last year—but the amount of out-relief is higher.

---

9. ***Extracts from a report on Gressenhall Workhouse by Sir John Walsham, poor law inspector, following his visit on 19 September 1866*** (Public Record Office, MH12 8482) Reports such as this, following routine visits to workhouses, were written under standard headings (in italics in the source above) on printed forms.

MITFORD AND LAUNDITCH UNION—All the fifty parishes of the Hundreds of Mitford and Launditch, were incorporated for the support of their poor, in 1775; but in 1801, the parish of East Dereham obtained an act by which it was separated from the incorporation. In 1836, the whole of these parishes, with ten parishes in Eynesford Hundred, were formed into an Union under the new poor law. These sixty parishes comprise an area of about 110,000 acres, and had in 1841 a population of 28,493 inhabitants, of whom 14,095 were males and 14,398 females. The House of Industry, which belonged to the old incorporation, is at Gressenhall, and was built in 1776 and '7, at the cost of £16,242, including the purchase of 61A. 2R. 35P. of land. In 1835, it was valued at nearly £10,000 and in the following year, about £5,000 was expended in repairs, alterations, &c, so as to adapt it as the Union Workhouse. The average annual expenditure of the sixty parishes of this extensive Union, from 1832 to 1835, was £26,684. In 1842, their expenditure, solely for the relief of in and out-door poor, was £9,815, and in 1843, £9,021. The number of persons in the workhouse, in July, 1841, was 242. On March 18th, 1844, there were 320 paupers in the house; and at one period in 1800, it had as many as 670 inmates. They are maintained and clothed at the weekly cost of 2s 4d per head. Though this large Workhouse stands in a high and healthy situation, cholera and scarlet fever, in 1834, swept away one-sixth of its inmates. Part of the land is enclosed as a burial ground, and the rest is cultivated by spade husbandry. Mr George Fras. and Mrs Whelan are master and matron of the workhouse; Mr Chas. Wright, of Litcham, is clerk to the Board of Guardians; the Rev. Jph. Thompson is chaplain; and Messrs Fras. Reynolds, Thos. Mendham, and John Francis Reynolds, are the relieving officers ...

10. *Extract concerning Mitford and Launditch Union from* **White's Directory of Norfolk,** *1845*

Riot in the Depwade Union—On Tuesday se'nnight, a large number of the inmates of the Depwade Union were brought before the Rev. Thos Howes and Wm Gwynn, Esq., at Pulham Saint Mary, charged with riotous conduct in the workhouse. The paupers had been all at dinner in the dining-hall on the previous Sunday, when, on a signal given, they rose simultaneously, and attempted to break open the bread-stores. They had three doors to break open before they got to the stores; two of which they succeeded in opening, and injured the third, when they were opposed by the master and other officers; and the police constables of the district were sent for to quell the disturbances.—After lengthened investigations, thirteen of the ringleaders were committed to Norwich Castle, for various periods of imprisonment; two for seven days, three for 21 days, three for 35 days, three for six weeks, and two for two months; and all to hard labour.

11. ***Riot in the Depwade Union*** (*Norfolk Chronicle*, 2 January 1847) Pulham Market Workhouse was one of several in Norfolk in which there were disturbances during the 'hungry forties'. There is no record of a major riot having taken place at Gressenhall Workhouse.

III
THEMES FOR INVESTIGATION

The ways in which a union workhouse is investigated by students will depend a great deal on the context in which the investigation takes place. Among the factors which will be influential are:

* the age of the students
* the curricular context, and in particular the relationship, if any, of the investigation to coverage of National Curriculum history
* the nature of the workhouse site, and whether a visit to the site is possible
* the extent to which the other sources described in the previous section can be made available to students

The investigations suggested in this section are therefore no more than suggestions, to be adapted in the light of circumstances. Gressenhall Workhouse in Norfolk, which has been investigated by large numbers of history students of all ages since the late 1970s, has been taken as the example, but most of the ideas will be transferable to other situations.

Changes in the Workhouse Buildings

This theme will involve looking for evidence of change over time on the site of a workhouse, using a range of sources including, if possible, the site itself. An alternative approach, not explored in detail here, would be to study several different workhouses whose buildings were erected at different dates.

i) Investigation away from the site

Whether or not a site visit is possible, much can be found out from a range of other sources about changes to the workhouse site. Good starting points might be the sources which provide basic information about the dates of construction of the buildings, and of additions and alterations to them. Such information is likely to be available in directories and, in more detail, in the registers of workhouse expenditure in class MH34 in the Public Record Office. In the case of Gressenhall Workhouse, combining the information from these two sources would give the following skeleton which chronology provides a framework to which evidence from other sources can be related:

1776-7:	Gressenhall House of Industry built at a cost of £16,242
1837:	£4,800 borrowed to pay for alteration and enlargement of the workhouse carried out in 1835-6
1871:	£2,000 borrowed to pay for alterations and additions at the workhouse
1901:	£3,650 borrowed to pay for alterations and additions at the workhouse

It may also be useful at an early stage of the investigation to consider the evidence provided by maps and plans of the site from different dates. Through comparison it should be possible to reach provisional conclusions about the approximate dates for the appearance and disappearance of the features marked, and then to relate these to the skeleton chronology already worked out.

Thus, for example, comparison of the first and second editions of the Ordnance Survey maps showing Gressenhall Workhouse will reveal that they are not identical: a few of the features shown in 1906 were not shown in 1883/4. The reliability of Ordnance Survey maps is not absolute, but they are unlikely to contain major errors. The reliability of other maps and plans may be variable. If comparison is made of the first edition of the Ordnance Survey map and an enclosure map, for example, allowance may need to be made for the possible unreliability of the latter.

Students might be asked to:
* arrange the maps in chronological sequence
* assess the reliability of each map
* identify the changes which, on the evidence available so far, have taken place on the site at different stages in its history
* discuss when the most significant changes took place

12. (Opposite top) *Enclosure map of Gressenhall, 1813* (Norfolk Record Office). This is an enlarged and adapted tracing of the part of the map which shows the house of industry.

13. (Opposite bottom) *Plan of Gressenhall Workhouse, 10 September 1849* (Public Record Office, MH12 8478) This was sent to the Poor Law Board by the Rev. Benjamin Barker, one of the Mitford and Launditch guardians. It was accompanied by a long letter, one of a series from Barker describing the drainage arrangements at the workhouse (see Source 37 for extracts from an earlier letter in the series). The dotted lines between pencilled letters B and E marked an open sewer. Although the workhouse buildings are not shown in great detail, this little plan is nevertheless a useful source. Comparison with Source 14 will suggest some of the changes which took place between 1849 and 1882-3, while comparison with Source 12 will provide an indication of the immediate impact on the site of the Poor Law Amendment Act of 1834.

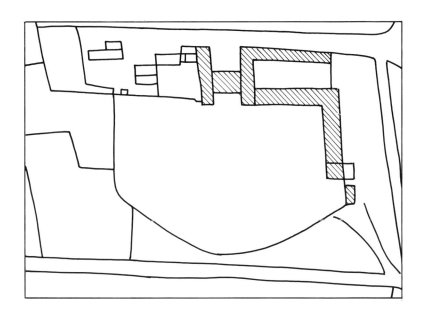

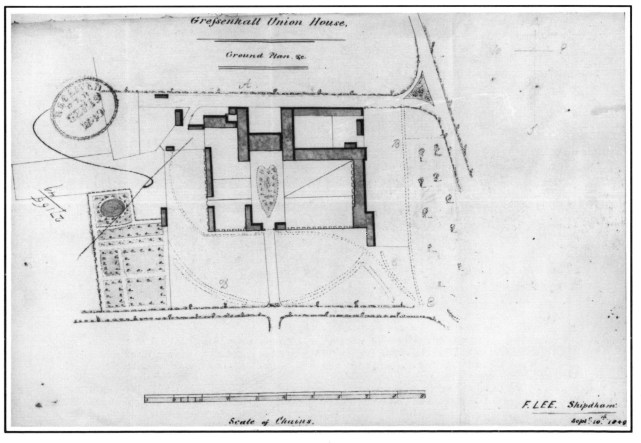

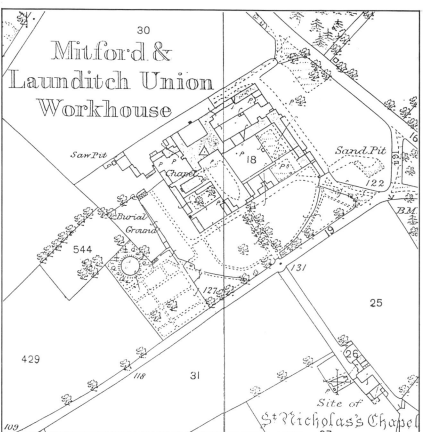

14. *Ordnance Survey 1:2,500 map, first edition* Gressenhall Workhouse lies on the boundary between two sheets of the map; the eastern sheet was surveyed in 1882 (published 1883), and the western in 1883 (published 1884).

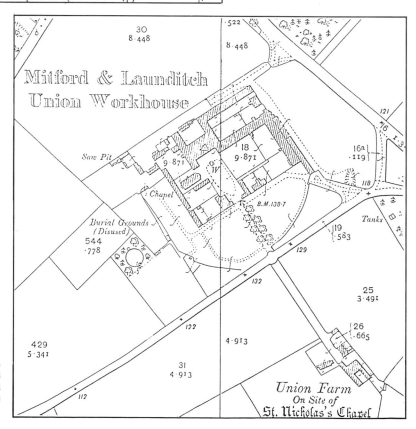

15. *Ordnance Survey 1:2,500 map, second edition* Revision of the western sheet took place in 1904, with the eastern sheet following in 1905. Both were published in 1906.

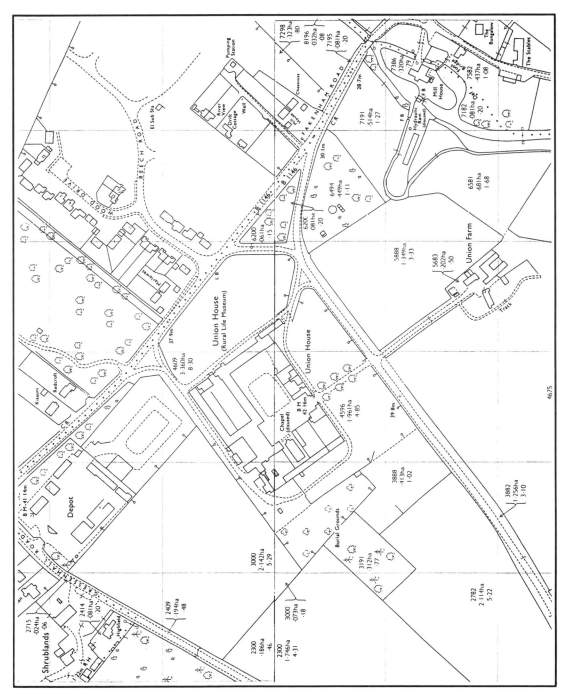

16. *Ordnance Survey 1:2,500 map, 1980 edition* This is based on a survey carried out in 1966, with a further revision in 1978. It shows the site as it was when acquired by the Norfolk Museums Service.

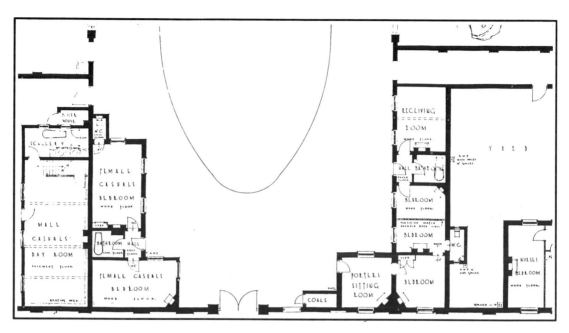

17. *Extract from a plan of Gressenhall Workhouse, 1930* (Norfolk Museums Service: Gressenhall Museum)
This plan of what was then known as Gressenhall Poor Law Institution was made by Norfolk County Council
when it assumed responsibility for the buildings, after the dissolution of the Mitford and Launditch board
of guardians. It is the only surviving plan which shows the internal organisation of the workhouse buildings.
This extract shows the area around the front gate.

The evidence of maps and plans may be supplemented by that from the visual sources
which may be available, as indicated in Section 2. In the case of Gressenhall Workhouse,
the survival of a painting of 1810 which shows the buildings as they were before the
passing of the 1834 Poor Law Amendment Act and the consequent modifications is
particularly fortunate. There is also a postcard dating from the turn of the century, and
some photographs dating from various dates in the late nineteenth and twentieth centuries,
of which two examples are included here. The value of these sources arises partly from the
fact that they show elevations, converting the two dimensional picture obtained from maps
and plans into a three dimensional one.

Students might be asked to:

* assess the reliability of each visual source
* compare the visual sources with the maps, matching the features shown with those
    shown on the maps and plans
* work out approximate dates for undated visual sources by comparing them with the
    maps and plans. If the dates are known (as they are in the case of Gressenhall),
    use the visual sources to assess the reliability of the maps and plans
* consider what can be learned from the visual sources about the nature of the changes
    which took place on the site

18. *Gressenhall House of Industry*, by Robert Kerrison, 1810 (Norfolk Museums Service: Gressenhall Museum) This painting shows the front of the building before the erection of the boundary wall. The arched arcade in the eastern wing is clearly visible (see Source 3). On the left is a windmill (which appears to have lost its sails) where corn was ground into flour for consumption in the house of industry and for sale. The windmill was sold and removed in 1837.

19. *Postcard showing the south eastern wing, Gressenhall Workhouse* (Norfolk Museums Service: Gressenhall Museum) The card is postmarked 1906. It shows the alterations to this wing which were completed by 1902. The 'sheds against the sick wards', the removal of which was called for by the inspector, Mr Bagenal, in 1897 (Source 80) are visible; one of them is still there today (Source 4). The name 'Beach Hill House' cannot be explained with certainty.

20. *Children in the infants' yard, c.1935-6* (Norfolk Museums Service: Gressenhall Museum). This photograph shows an internal dividing wall (dating from 1871) which has now been removed. These children were probably 'boarded out' or transferred to a children's home when they were older. A swing was referred to in the minutes of the meeting of the board of guardians on 16 January 1843: 'Resolved that a Tree upon the Farm be taken down for the purpose of erecting a swing for the children'.

21. *The front yard, Gressenhall Workhouse, c.1917-8* (Norfolk Museums Service: Gressenhall Museum) By the time this photograph was taken, railings had partly replaced some of the high walls which divided the different exercise yards. Both they and the well house have now gone. The man in the foreground is the porter, Mr Bilham. A former inmate whose childhood was spent in the workhouse recently recalled Bilham as a hard, unsympathetic man who scrubbed him with carbolic soap until his skin was raw.

The next step could be to turn to some of the documentary and printed sources already described, which contain evidence relating to changes in the workhouse site and buildings. Entries in the minute books of the board of guardians may enable more precise dates to be given for some of the changes already identified from other sources. So also will items in the poor law union papers, the volumes of correspondence in class MH12 in the Public Record Office (henceforward referred to as the 'MH12 correspondence') and, on occasion, reports or advertisements in the local newspapers. Such sources will also provide more evidence about the initial construction of the workhouse and the detailed nature of subsequent additions and alterations. They may provide valuable references to surviving features on the site.

Some changes of a more minor nature, such as alterations in the use to which different parts of the buildings were put, may be learned about only from the documentary and printed sources. Crucially, these sources will also provide insights into the reasons for changes and, in some cases, the debates which preceded or accompanied them. There may also be evidence about changes considered but not made, and the reasons for these decisions.

Students might be asked to:

* compare the evidence from documentary and printed sources with that from the other
  sources
* consider the extent to which the documentary sources assist interpretation of the
  changes identifiable from the other sources

---

1. To alter and adapt the upper story of the two adjacent east wings and the ground
   story of one of them as wards for the ordinary sick.
2. To re-appropriate and make various slight alterations in certain other parts of the
   House necessitated by alteration No.1.
3. To erect new itch and receiving wards. And
4. To erect new detached infectious wards.

---

22. *Details of proposed alterations and additions to Gressenhall Workhouse, filed by the Poor Law Board on 25 March 1871* (Public Record Office, MH12 8483)

Mitford and Launditch Union

TO BUILDERS AND ENGINEERS

The Guardians of the above Union invite TENDERS for Alterations and New Structural Works, Hot Water Heating, Supply by Rain and Storage of Water, Engineering Works, including Boilers, Cooking Apparatus, Laundry Machinery, Pumping Engines, and Iron Emergency Staircase, &c at their Workhouse, at Gressenhall, in accordance with the Plans and Specifications, which may be seen on application to Mr John B Pearce, F.R.I.B.A., Upper King Street, Norwich.
Sealed Tenders endorsed "Workhouse Alterations" or "Heating" or "Boilers" &c as the case may be, to be sent to me at the Guildhall, East Dereham, on or before the 25th instant.
The Guardians do not bind themselves to accept the Lowest or any Tender.

WALTER M BARTON
Clerk to the Guardians

The Guildhall, East Dereham
4th September, 1901

---

23. *Invitation to tender for works at Gressenhall Workhouse* (*Eastern Daily Press*, 9 September 1901)

ii) Investigation on site

If it is possible, investigation on site is desirable both because it stimulates students' interest and increases their enjoyment and motivation, and because it enables them to explore issues relating to the development of the site in a way which is not possible at second hand. If it is not possible, however, use could be made of video, slides or photographs such as those included in this section (or, if the facilities are available, CD ROM) as means of providing some contact with the physical evidence offered by the workhouse buildings, yards and grounds. Examination of building materials and architectural styles will enable an approximate date to be suggested for some of the features. The site will also, almost inevitably, provide evidence of change: of the removal of features, the adding of new ones, and the adaptation of surviving ones. This evidence may make it possible to suggest a sequence for the surviving features. Cross-referencing with the other sources available should enable students to use the non-physical evidence to interpret the physical evidence and vice versa.

In order to identify and interpret relevant evidence on site, students may require specific background knowledge and interpretative skills. At Gressenhall, for example, as a general rule the brickwork of the 18th-century buildings is in English bond while that of the 19th-century buildings is in Flemish bond. There are also several places where it is apparent that changes have been made: where bricks laid later butt up against earlier work, or where later features cut across earlier ones. An example of the latter is where a roof abuts against a wall, partially covering blocked up windows in the wall. There may be specific clues which will enable hypotheses to be advanced about the uses of different parts of the site and buildings. For example, the discovery of an outbuilding divided into a series of small cells might suggest that this part of the site provided accommodation for vagrants. At Gressenhall, surviving features include a mortuary and the hooks to which the guardians' horses were tethered when they came to the workhouse for their Monday morning meetings.

Ideally, investigation of the evidence offered by the workhouse site would go hand in hand with investigation of the other sources available, with each helping to inform and suggest questions for the other. In the real world, any time which students are able to spend on site is likely to be limited—it may be confined to a single day. In these circumstances, thought will need to be given to the relationship between the on-site and off-site investigations.

On the one hand, investigation on site could be used primarily as a stimulus for further investigation off site. Students would perhaps be given some general background on the poor law but very little specific information about the site before their visit. During the visit there could be a broad brief, with the emphasis on open-minded observation and the framing of questions for further investigation later from the other sources available.

Students might be asked to:

* look for and record similarities and differences, in terms of building styles and materials, between the various parts of the site
* look for and record evidence of change and of the dates or sequence of different features
* suggest which features date from after 1930, which from the original construction of the workhouse, and which from the intervening period
* use fragmentary surviving evidence to infer the existence of features which have largely disappeared
* speculate about possible uses of different parts of the site

Alternatively, the time spent on site could come towards the end of the investigation. Students would arrive with a developed view of the history of the site based on their investigation of the other sources. The visit could involve a focus on specific questions or hypotheses arising from the earlier work. As well as carrying out the tasks suggested above, students might be asked to:

* match features with those shown on the maps and in visual sources and referred to in the documentary and printed sources
* consider the extent to which the evidence on site either confirms or challenges hypotheses about the site's development which may have been developed already
* identify any additional evidence about the development of the site which does not match that already acquired from other sources
* reach conclusions about the development of the site and consider the reliability of those conclusions

In practice, perhaps, many visits will combine elements from both approaches. As always, how the investigation is organised will depend crucially on the ages of the students, the curricular context, and the nature of the site and the other sources being used. In general it will probably be desirable to avoid over-dominance of the 'guided tour' approach: though this might enable students to acquire plenty of information about the site and form a strong impression of what it might have been like in the past, it is unlikely to help them to reflect upon the evidence and pursue the investigation for themselves.

24. *Section of the east wing, Gressenhall Workhouse* (Andy Reid) The wall is built in English bond up to the bottoms of the first-floor windows; the remainder is in Flemish bond. Comparison with Source 18 confirms that only the ground floor formed part of the original 18th-century buildings: the first floor was probably added in 1836-7.

25. *The north east wing of the central block, Gressenhall Workhouse* (Andy Reid) Part of the wall of the main 18th-century building collapsed during the alterations of 1836-7 and had to be reconstructed. This work was done in Flemish bond. Later, probably in the period 1895-1902, a lean-to containing toilets was erected against the rebuilt wall; this involved blocking up two of the windows. The single-storey building to the right is the laundry, which also dates from the period 1895-1902.

26. *The front gate and porter's lodge, Gressenhall Workhouse* (Norfolk Museums Service: Andy Reid) This part of the workhouse site provides plenty of evidence of a complicated building history. A blocked-up door and a blocked-up window, for example, are visible in the photograph. Comparison with Sources 13, 14, 15 and 17 helps to unravel the sequence of changes, but does not resolve all of the problems posed by the physical evidence.

27. (Left) *Brickwork in the front yard, Gressenhall Workhouse* (Andy Reid) This is where the dividing wall (and, later, the railings seen in Source 21) joined the corner of the eastern front wing of the main building.

28. (Right) *Doorway in the east wing, Gressenhall Workhouse* (Andy Reid) Here, in the north wall of the eastern wing, the development of the building can be related concisely and effectively to the broader historical context. The generously-proportioned window set in the 18th-century wall of the house of industry (in English bond) was bricked up (in Flemish bond) in 1836-7 on the express instructions of the assistant poor law commissioner, Dr James Kay, to create a refractory cell in the space behind it—one of the measures taken to enforce strict discipline under the new poor law. Later (probably in the period 1895-1902) the refractory cell, which was no longer considered necessary, was converted into a wash-house for men, with a new doorway providing communication with the exercise yard outside.

29. *South-eastern corner of the workhouse site* (Andy Reid) On the left is the fever ward, built in 1871 and referred to in Source 22 as the 'new detached infectious wards'. The iron emergency staircase mentioned in Source 23 can be seen leading down from the doorway on the first floor of the south-eastern wing.

iii) Relating the site to poor law history

The emphasis in this part of the investigation will be on explaining (rather than just reconstructing) the changes which have taken place on the site. One approach might be to relate changes in the workhouse buildings to the local and national factors which brought about or influenced those changes. Alternatively, the starting point could be the developments which took place at the national level, and the investigation could focus on the extent to which these were reflected in the workhouse buildings being studied. As already mentioned, documentary and printed sources may shed light on the specific reasons for changes, and thereby reveal the links between national and local developments. It was the assistant poor law commissioner or poor law inspector who generally represented national perspectives to the guardians, and his influence may be recorded in the sources.

Students might be asked to:

* explain the changes in the workhouse site and buildings which took place over time
* consider the extent to which the changes reflected changes in policy nationally
* consider the extent to which the changes reflected specific local factors or circumstances
* assess the role of the assistant poor law commissioners and poor law inspectors in bringing about the changes
* assess the extent to which the changes at the workhouse investigated were typical of those which took place across the country

In the case of Gressenhall Workhouse, the relationship between changes in the site and buildings and national developments could be expressed in the table below:

Gressenhall	**National Developments**
Construction of the original buildings 1776-7	Local control, and comparatively generous attitudes to poor relief in the second half of the 18th century
Alterations and additions, 1836-7; creation of walled exercise yards	Implementation of the Poor Law Amendment Act of 1834; more punitive attitude
Building of separate ward for elderly respectable married couples, 1853	Slight softening of attitudes in the mid 19th century
Conversion of one wing into infirmary; erection of detached fever ward, 1870-1	Medical advances; campaign of *The Lancet* and others for improvements in workhouse infirmaries in the late 1860s
Improvements in the infirmary, laundry and kitchens; central heating system and new system of drains installed, 1895-1902	Further advances in medicine and public health. Further softening of attitudes to poor relief and greater public accountability of boards of guardians
Demolition of many internal walls; creation of lawns, flower beds, etc, 1930-1974.	Transfer of workhouses to county councils, 1930; end of poor law, 1948; conversion to old people's home
Repointing, replacement of brickwork, repairs, erection of new building, etc.	Changing ideas on provision for old people; conversion to museum from 1976

Life in the Union Workhouse

Investigation of this theme will involve use of a range of sources to reconstruct workhouse life, including not only the workings of the institution but also the everyday lives and attitudes of workhouse inmates and officers.

i) Daily routine

A good starting point for investigating the daily routine of the union workhouse is the formal framework of regulations provided by the central authority. For the mid-19th century reference should be made to the General Order (Consolidated) of 1847, which sets out regulations for the 'government of the workhouse' with a detailed commentary. Among the matters dealt with are the admission and reception of inmates, classification, discipline, diet and the punishments to be used. Further evidence on how the regulations were applied, and on daily life generally in the workhouse being studied, will come from the minute books of the board of guardians, the MH12 correspondence, local newspapers and on occasion from other sources. For Gressenhall Workhouse, the guidance for workhouse masters and matrons issued by the poor law inspector Sir John Walsham in 1861, from class MH32 in the Public Record Office, is a particularly useful source in this connection.

References to the actual procedures used when inmates were admitted or discharged may occasionally be found in the minute books and MH12 correspondence, and details of their reception into the workhouse may be gleaned from these and other sources (including oral testimony—see source 77). Details of the clothing which was issued to new inmates when they had surrendered their own clothes are usually frustratingly elusive, but there may be a few references in the minute books and the MH12 correspondence. Further clues may be found in newspaper advertisements seeking tenders for the supply of the materials from which the workhouse clothes were made. In the case of Gressenhall Workhouse, additional evidence comes from an unusual source—three dolls dating from the first half of the present century which are dressed in 'workhouse clothes'.

On admission, inmates were placed in 'receiving wards' where they were 'classified', after which they were transferred to the part of the workhouse set aside for their class. If there are large scale plans of the site, they will probably show how the sleeping quarters, day rooms and yards were allocated to the various classes. There may be occasional references in the minute books and MH12 correspondence to changes in the fine detail of the classification, and other evidence from the same sources may indicate how rigidly or otherwise the separation of the classes was maintained in practice.

Some idea of the nature of the workhouse environment and the kinds of facilities available will undoubtedly be gained from the surviving buildings and yards. These may also convey something of the 'atmosphere' of the institution. The minute books, MH12 correspondence, and other sources will yield evidence about matters such as the arrangements for heating, washing, laundry and sanitation. References to epidemics may enable more to be inferred about the overall sanitary condition of the institution. The arrangements in the dormitories, and the kinds of beds and mattresses used, may also be mentioned.

References to the whitewashing and 'colouring' of walls and the maintenance of floors may enable some idea of the internal appearance of the rooms to be obtained. There may, similarly, be clues to the appearance of the yards. At Gressenhall they were gravelled and had privies which were sometimes malodorous; but in the old men's yard, surprisingly, a vine grew. Births (in most cases to unmarried women) and deaths were regular events in the life of the workhouse, and the minute books and MH12 correspondence may contain references to the arrangements made when they took place.

Details of the daily routine may be obtained from regulations setting out the hours of work and meal and bed times; these may be found in the MH12 correspondence. The correspondence and the minute books may also contain occasional references to the actual work done by the inmates and to the limited opportunities for recreation which were available to them. Arrangements for religious observance may also be mentioned. Records of what was considered to be disorderly or refractory behaviour by inmates, and the punishments imposed, are among the commonest entries in the minute books, and they provide an indication of the strictness of workhouse discipline. The existence of a punishment book will obviate the need to search through the minutes for this type of information.

The diet for inmates of different classes was set out in dietaries, printed or otherwise, which should be found among the national or local records. Further evidence can be gained from newspaper advertisements seeking tenders for the supply of foodstuffs, and occasional references in the minute books and MH12 correspondence. Departures from the normal dietary regime were rare and, whether occasioned by Christmas or by some other special event, were generally recorded in the minutes. On occasion they were reported in the local newspapers as well.

Students might be asked to:

* reconstruct in as much detail as possible an average day in the life of a workhouse inmate
* make a judgment on the extent to which life for workhouse inmates was harsh, and identify the particular features which made it so
* consider the reliability of the judgment they have made, and suggest further evidence which might enable them to increase its reliability

---

Art.98.—The paupers, so far as the Workhouse admits therof, shall be classed as follows:
Class 1.   Men infirm through age or any other cause.
Class 2.   Able-bodied men and youths above the age of fifteen years.
Class 3.   Boys above the age of seven years, and under that of fifteen.
Class 4.   Women infirm through age or any other cause.
Class 5.   Able-bodied women and girls above the age of fifteen years.
Class 6.   Girls above the age of seven years, and under that of fifteen.
Class 7.   Children under seven years of age.

---

31. *Article 98, General Order (Consolidated), 24 July 1847*

Art.91.—As soon as the pauper is admitted, he shall be placed in some room to be appropriated to the reception of paupers on admission, and shall then be examined by the Medical Officer.

Art.92.—If the Medical Officer, upon such examination, pronounce the pauper to be labouring under any disease of body or mind, the pauper shall be placed in the sick ward or in such other ward as the Medical Officer shall direct.

Art.93.—If the Medical Officer pronounce the pauper to be free from any such disease, the pauper shall be placed in the part of the Workhouse assigned to the class to which he may belong ...

Art.95.—Before being removed from the receiving ward, the pauper shall be thoroughly cleansed, and shall be clothed in a Workhouse dress, and the clothes which he wore at the time of his admission shall be purified and deposited in a place appropriated for that purpose, with the pauper's name affixed thereto. Such clothes shall be restored to the pauper when he leaves the Workhouse.

Art.96.—Every pauper shall, upon his admission into the Workhouse, be searched by or under the inspection of the proper officer, and all articles prohibited by any Act of Parliament, or by this Order, which may be found upon his person, shall be taken from him, and, so far as may be proper, restored to him at his Departure from the Workhouse.

30. *Articles 91-93 and 95-96, General Order (Consolidated), 24 July 1847*

Art.127. Any pauper, being an inmate of the Workhouse, who shall neglect to observe such of the regulations in this Order as are applicable to him as such inmate;—

Or who shall make any noise when silence is ordered to be kept;

Or shall use obscene or profane language;

Or shall by word or deed insult or revile any person;

Or shall threaten to strike or to assault any person;

Or shall not duly cleanse his person;

Or shall refuse or neglect to work, after having been required to do so;

Or shall pretend sickness;

Or shall play at cards or other games of chance;

Or shall refuse to go into his proper ward or yard, or shall enter, or attempt to enter, without permission, the ward or yard appropriated to any class of paupers other than that to which he belongs;

Or shall climb over any fence or boundary wall surrounding any portion of the Workhouse premises, or shall attempt to leave the Workhouse otherwise than through the ordinary entrance;

Or shall misbehave in going to, at, or returning from Public Worship out of the Workhouse, or at Divine Service or Prayers in the Workhouse;

Or, having received temporary leave of absence, and wearing the Workhouse clothes, shall return to the Workhouse after the appointed time of absence, without reasonable cause for delay;

Or shall wilfully disobey any lawful order of any officer of the Workhouse;

Shall be deemed DISORDERLY.

Art.128.—Any pauper, being an inmate of the Workhouse, who shall, within seven days, repeat any one, or commit more than one, of the offences specified in Art.127;

Or who shall by word or deed insult or revile the Master or Matron, or any other Officer of the Workhouse, or any of the Guardians;

Or shall wilfully disobey any lawful order of the Master or Matron, after such order shall have been repeated;

(continued overleaf)

Or shall unlawfully strike or otherwise unlawfully assault any person;
Or shall wilfully or mischievously damage or soil any property whatsoever belonging to the Guardians;
Or shall wilfully waste or spoil any provisions, stock, tools, or materials for work belonging to the Guardians;
Or shall be drunk;   Or shall wilfully disturb other persons at Public Worship out of the Workhouse, or at Divine Service or Prayers in the Workhouse;
Shall be deemed REFRACTORY.

Art.129.—The Master may, with or without the Direction of the Guardians, punish any disorderly pauper by substituting during a time not greater than forty-eight hours, for his dinner, as prescribed by the Dietary, a meal consisting of eight ounces of bread, or one pound of cooked potatoes or boiled rice, and also by withholding from him, during the same period, all butter, cheese, tea, sugar, or broth, which such pauper would otherwise receive, at any meal during the time aforesaid.
Art.130.—The Guardians may, by a special direction to be entered on their minutes, order any refractory pauper to be punished by confinement in a separate room, with or without an alteration of diet, similar in kind and duration to that prescribed in Art.129 for disorderly paupers; but no pauper shall be so confined for a longer period than twenty-four hours; or, if it be deemed right that such pauper should be carried before a Justice of the Peace, and if such period of twenty-four hours should be insufficient for that purpose, than for such further time as may be necessary for such purpose.

32. *Articles 127-130, General Order (Consolidated), 24 July 1847*

Memoranda for the Guidance of Masters and Matrons on Workhouses in Sir John Walsham's District
1. The first care of the Master and Matron (after providing adequately for the necessary wants in the several wards under their superintendance) should be to select from among the inmates a suitable Wardsman or Wardswoman who should be held at all times responsible to the Master and Matron for the cleanliness and order of their respective wards. Whenever any neglect or inattention on their parts appear, they should be admonished; and if after admonition any Wardsman or Wardswoman persists in neglecting, or in allowing the other inmates to disregard the rules of the ward, it will be the Master or Matron's duty to remove that person from his or her post—or if need be to deal with his or her disobedience of orders according to the punishment regulations. Strict observance of this rule and diligent personal supervision, on the part of the Master or Matron, are essential to secure systematic regularity.
2. Particular attention must be paid to the enforcement of tidiness and cleanliness in the day wards and especially in the day rooms of the able-bodied women with children and of the old men, whose wards it is usually the most difficult to keep in the order necessary in all public establishments.
3. In all the day rooms, but especially in those just particularized, it is essential that nothing should be allowed to be littered about. The Master and Matron having satisfied themselves (see section 1) as to what is really necessary for the use and permissible comforts of the inmates, should at once, and from time to time, remove all that is in their opinion superfluous.
4. What articles of necessity (and they should be very few in number) the Master and Matron may allow to remain, must, when not actually in use, be placed neatly away in cupboards to be provided

(*continued opposite*)

for the purpose, such cupboards being unfailingly subjected to the close daily inspection of the Master and Matron, so as to ensure their being kept perfectly clean. It will, however, require constant watchfulness on the part of the Master and Matron to prevent the cupboards becoming receptacles of dirt; and particularly to prevent candles, bottles, tins &c being placed on top of, instead of within, the cupboards.

5. In making their daily visits to the day rooms, the Master and Matron will also take care to see that the stove or fire places, and the fire-irons have been properly cleaned, and all cobwebs removed. In additions to the cleaning of cupboards due regard should likewise be paid to the cleaning of benches, rubbing of chairs, and scrubbing of floors in all the wards. Whilst to prevent hats, bonnets or caps from lying about, a hat rack should be provided in each ward.

6. The beds should at all times present an appearance of scrupulous neatness. The sheets, throughout every room, except when the windows are open on damp days, should be turned down to an uniform depth, and the rugs should hang uniformly both at the sides and foot of the bed. The chamber utensils should be washed every morning with a cloth and cold water and daily deposited, if possible, in a cupboard. Much care is also required, in sweeping bed-room floors, and in dusting ledges, windows, &c.

7. Neither in the day rooms, nor the bed rooms, are bonnets, boxes, or any other property of the inmates to be allowed on any pretence whatever. All the property of the inmates must be duly cleansed, ticketed and put away in the store-room; where, however, the inmates may be permitted, from time to time, to see what belongs to them, if they wish it.

8. Neither must the inmates be suffered, under any excuse whatever, to carry food away into their bedrooms— though the Matron will, of course, see that milk and bread and any other article of food *absolutely required* for the infants may be kept in sufficient quantities in the women's day room; great care and firmness, however, must be shewn by the Matron on this point—otherwise able-bodied women under the pretext of obtaining and keeping food for their infants, will infallibly make their day-room and its cupboards a perfect nuisance from accumulations of stale food &c. Cooking or tea-making in any of the day-rooms of the house is most undesirable—trafficking in provisions must be strictly prohibited—and, in all cases, when a pauper cannot consume his allowance of food it should (if practicable) be returned to the stores.

9. The Matron must take care that every attention is paid by the nurses to the sick paupers. The helpless should have their persons daily cleansed for them, and their hair combed. The sheets used for the sick wards should be changed every fortnight as a general rule, but oftener if necessary; and as it will frequently happen, that extra changes of linen will be required, a certain number of shirts, not numbered in the ordinary way, but called (say) "lending shirts", should be provided. Chloride of lime should be frequently used in the sick apartments, and unremitting attention paid to their ventilation and cleanliness.

10. The whole of the children in the workhouse should be washed in a bath with warm water and soap every Saturday afternoon under the superintendence of the Schoolmaster and Schoolmistress. The adults also should be provided with tubs and warm water and soap in their wards on the Saturday evening. And the Master and the Matron should insist upon their only cleansing their persons (unless otherwise directed by the Medical Officer) on these occasions. Combs and brushes should be provided for every ward.

33. *Memoranda for the Guidance of Masters and Matrons of Workhouses in Sir John Walsham's District, 1861* (Public Record Office, MH32 84)

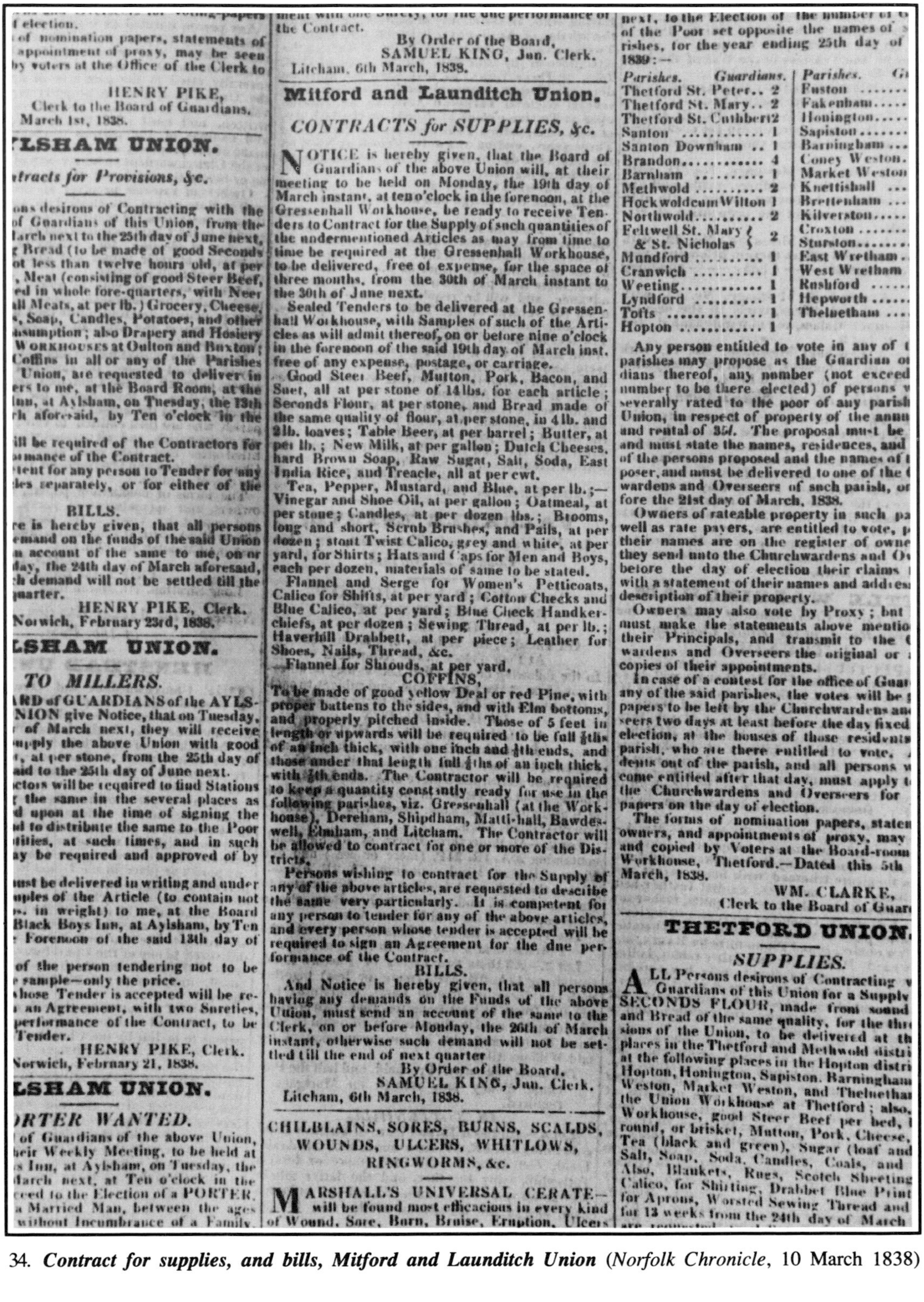

f election.
of nomination papers, statements of
appointment of proxy, may be seen
by voters at the Office of the Clerk to

HENRY PIKE,
Clerk to the Board of Guardians,
March 1st, 1838.

LSHAM UNION.

tracts for Provisions, &c.

ons desirous of Contracting with the
of Guardians of this Union, from the
arch next to the 25th day of June next,
g Bread (to be made of good Seconds
ot less than twelve hours old, at per
, Meat (consisting of good Steer Beef,
ed in whole fore-quarters, with Neer
all Meats, at per lb.) Grocery, Cheese,
s, Soap, Candles, Potatoes, and other
sumption; also Drapery and Hosiery
WORKHOUSES at Oulton and Buxton;
Coffins in all or any of the Parishes
Union, are requested to deliver in
rs to me, at the Board Room, at the
Inn, at Aylsham, on Tuesday, the 13th
rh aforesaid, by Ten o'clock in the

ill be required of the Contractors for
umance of the Contract.
tent for any person to Tender for any
les separately, or for either of the

BILLS.
re is hereby given, that all persons
emand on the funds of the said Union
n account of the same to me, on or
day, the 24th day of March aforesaid,
ch demand will not be settled till the
quarter.
HENRY PIKE, Clerk.
Norwich, February 23rd, 1838.

LSHAM UNION.

TO MILLERS.

ARD of GUARDIANS of the AYLS-
NION give Notice, that on Tuesday,
r of March next, they will receive
upply the above Union with good
, at per stone, from the 25th day of
aid to the 25th day of June next.
ctors will be required to find Stations
the same in the several places as
d upon at the time of signing the
al to distribute the same to the Poor
lities, at such times, and in such
ay be required and approved of by

ust be delivered in writing and under
uples of the Article (to contain not
s. in weight) to me, at the Board
Black Boys Inn, at Aylsham, by Ten
: Forenoon of the said 13th day of

of the person tendering not to be
: sample—only the price.
hose Tender is accepted will be re-
: an Agreement, with two Sureties,
performance of the Contract, to be
Tender.
HENRY PIKE, Clerk.
Norwich, February 21, 1838.

LSHAM UNION.

ORTER WANTED.

of Guardians of the above Union,
heir Weekly Meeting, to be held at
s Inn, at Aylsham, on Tuesday, the
March next, at Ten o'clock in the
ceed to the Election of a PORTER,
a Married Man, between the ages
without Incumbrance of a Family.

---

meat with one Surety, for the due performance of
the Contract.
By Order of the Board,
SAMUEL KING, Jun. Clerk.
Litcham, 6th March, 1838.

Mitford and Launditch Union.

CONTRACTS for SUPPLIES, &c.

NOTICE is hereby given, that the Board of
Guardians of the above Union will, at their
meeting to be held on Monday, the 19th day of
March instant, at ten o'clock in the forenoon, at the
Gressenhall Workhouse, be ready to receive Tenders to Contract for the Supply of such quantities of
the undermentioned Articles as may from time to
time be required at the Gressenhall Workhouse,
to be delivered, free of expense, for the space of
three months, from the 30th of March instant to
the 30th of June next.
Sealed Tenders to be delivered at the Gressenhall Workhouse, with Samples of such of the Articles as will admit thereof, on or before nine o'clock
in the forenoon of the said 19th day of March inst.
free of any expense, postage, or carriage.
Good Steer Beef, Mutton, Pork, Bacon, and
Suet, all at per stone of 14lbs. for each article;
Seconds Flour, at per stone, and Bread made of
the same quality of flour, at per stone, in 4lb. and
2lb. loaves; Table Beer, at per barrel; Butter, at
per lb.; New Milk, at per gallon; Dutch Cheeses,
hard Brown Soap, Raw Sugar, Salt, Soda, East
India Rice, and Treacle, all at per cwt.
Tea, Pepper, Mustard, and Blue, at per lb.;—
Vinegar and Shoe Oil, at per gallon; Oatmeal, at
per stone; Candles, at per dozen lbs.; Brooms,
long and short, Scrub Brushes, and Pails, at per
dozen; stout Twist Calico, grey and white, at per
yard, for Shirts; Hats and Caps for Men and Boys,
each per dozen; materials of same to be stated.
Flannel and Serge for Women's Petticoats,
Calico for Shifts, at per yard; Cotton Checks and
Blue Calico, at per yard; Blue Check Handker-
chiefs, at per dozen; Sewing Thread, at per lb.;
Haverhill Drabbett, at per piece; Leather for
Shoes, Nails, Thread, &c.
Flannel for Shrouds, at per yard,
COFFINS,
To be made of good yellow Deal or red Pine, with
proper battens to the sides, and with Elm bottoms,
and properly pitched inside. Those of 5 feet in
length or upwards will be required to be full ⅞ths
of an inch thick, with one inch and ⅜ths ends, and
those under that length full ⅝ths of an inch thick,
with ⅜th ends. The Contractor will be required
to keep a quantity constantly ready for use in the
following parishes, viz. Gressenhall (at the Workhouse), Dereham, Shipdham, Mattishall, Bawdes-
well, Elmham, and Litcham. The Contractor will
be allowed to contract for one or more of the Districts.
Persons wishing to contract for the Supply of
any of the above articles, are requested to describe
the same very particularly. It is competent for
any person to tender for any of the above articles,
and every person whose tender is accepted will be
required to sign an Agreement for the due performance of the Contract.
BILLS.
And Notice is hereby given, that all persons
having any demands on the Funds of the above
Union, must send an account of the same to the
Clerk, on or before Monday, the 26th of March
instant, otherwise such demand will not be settled till the end of next quarter.
By Order of the Board,
SAMUEL KING, Jun. Clerk.
Litcham, 6th March, 1838.

CHILBLAINS, SORES, BURNS, SCALDS,
WOUNDS, ULCERS, WHITLOWS,
RINGWORMS, &c.

MARSHALL'S UNIVERSAL CERATE—
will be found most efficacious in every kind
of Wound, Sore, Burn, Bruise, Eruption, Ulcer,

---

next, to the Election of the number of
of the Poor set opposite the names of
rishes, for the year ending 25th day of
1839:—

Parishes.	Guardians.	Parishes.	G
Thetford St. Peter..	2	Euston	
Thetford St. Mary..	2	Fakenham	
Thetford St. Cuthbert	2	Honington	
Santon	1	Sapiston	
Santon Downham ..	1	Barningham	
Brandon	4	Coney Weston..	
Barnham	1	Market Weston	
Methwold	2	Knettishall	
Hockwold cum Wilton	2	Brettenham	
Northwold	2	Kilverston....	
Feltwell St. Mary & St. Nicholas	2	Croxton	
		Sturston.....	
Mundford	1	East Wretham ..	
Cranwich	1	West Wretham	
Weeting	1	Rushford	
Lyndford	1	Hepworth	
Tofts	1	Thelnetham	
Hopton	1		

Any person entitled to vote in any of t
parishes may propose as the Guardian or
dians thereof, any number (not exceed
number to be there elected) of persons v
severally rated to the poor of any parish
Union, in respect of property of the annu
and rental of 35l. The proposal must be
and must state the names, residences, and
of the persons proposed and the names of t
poser, and must be delivered to one of the C
wardens and Overseers of such parish, or
fore the 21st day of March, 1838.
Owners of rateable property in such pa
well as rate payers, are entitled to vote, p
their names are on the register of owne
they send unto the Churchwardens and O
before the day of election their claims
with a statement of their names and addre
description of their property.
Owners may also vote by Proxy; but
must make the statements above mentio
their Principals, and transmit to the C
wardens and Overseers the original or
copies of their appointments.
In case of a contest for the office of Guar
any of the said parishes, the votes will be
papers to be left by the Churchwardens an
seers two days at least before the day fixed
election, at the houses of those residents
parish, who are there entitled to vote.
dents out of the parish, and all persons w
come entitled after that day, must apply to
the Churchwardens and Overseers for
papers on the day of election.
The forms of nomination papers, staten
owners, and appointments of proxy, may
and copied by Voters at the Board-room
Workhouse, Thetford.—Dated this 5th
March, 1838.
WM. CLARKE,
Clerk to the Board of Guar

THETFORD UNION.

SUPPLIES.

ALL Persons desirous of Contracting w
Guardians of this Union for a Supply
SECONDS FLOUR, made from sound
and Bread of the same quality, for the thr
sions of the Union, to be delivered at th
places in the Thetford and Methwold dist
at the following places in the Hopton distri
Hopton, Honington, Sapiston, Barningham
Weston, Market Weston, and Thelnethan
the Union Workhouse at Thetford; also,
Workhouse, good Steer Beef per bed,
round, or brisket, Mutton, Pork, Cheese,
Tea (black and green), Sugar (loaf and
Salt, Soap, Soda, Candles, Coals, and
Also, Blankets, Rugs, Scotch Sheeting
Calico, for Shirting, Drabbet Blue Print
for Aprons, Worsted Sewing Thread and
for 12 weeks from the 24th day of March

---

34. *Contract for supplies, and bills, Mitford and Launditch Union* (*Norfolk Chronicle*, 10 March 1838)

35. *Exercise yard* (Andy Reid) This lies to the north of the eastern wing of the workhouse, and this means that part of it is almost permanently in shadow. Until 1930 it was divided into two separate yards for men. Just visible on the right is the high wall which separates these from the laundry yard, where some of the women worked.

Ordered that five shillings be given to Mary Ann Nichols and Lucy Loveday for their services in the Union Workhouse in nursing 80 children sick in measels and typhus fever.

36. *Minute concerning payment for nursing* (minute book of the board of guardians of Mitford and Launditch Union, 5 August 1844: Norfolk Record Office C/GP14/6) The two women to whom payment was made were workhouse inmates. Sanitary conditions at Gressenhall Workhouse were not good—a large number of inmates had died in outbreaks of cholera and scarlet fever in 1834.

... Having, in consequence of advanced years (I enter my 72nd year this week) given up my attendance at the Board of Guardians for some time I was induced to resume it, about the middle of November last —because I found they were doing nothing towards improving the Sanitary state of the Union— Remembering that the cholera had been very fatal in the workhouse, now our Union house—on its last visit to this country, the first question I asked, was; whether anything could be done to improve its sanitary state by attention to the sewerage, ventilation or otherwise—and the answer I received from the chairman of the visiting committee (now the Chairman of the Board)—was, that everything was in a most perfect state—and, of course, that it was not capable of improvement—From subsequent enquiries, however, I found, that this representation was anything but correct— and that the privies, in two of the wards, were in a most horrid state—after repeated failures I did, at last, persuade the Guardians to make an inspection, by a deputation of their body, who reported that it was even so—but, notwithstanding their report, nothing was done for weeks, tho' an order was ultimately made for the nuisance being abated ...

—Besides this my own senses discovered another abominable nuisance. There is an open ditch running parallel with one wing of the house, at about five and twenty yards distance, into which all the drains of the house empty themselves— the length of this drain is more than 150 yards—the effluvium from this must necessarily be injurious to health—but tho' I have repeatedly—and at the urgent request of the Surgeon of the house, recommended this ditch to be converted into a covered drain—which might be done for about £20—I have, as repeatedly, been outvoted ...

37. *Extracts from a letter from the Rev. Benjamin Barker to the Poor Law Board, 7 June 1849* (Public Record Office, MH12 8478) This is one of a series of letters written by Barker (see also Source 13), whose tenacity in exposing 'nuisances' and advocating sanitary improvements alienated him from the other guardians. They, according to the poor law inspector Sir John Walsham, looked upon 'Mr Barker ... as himself the greatest of nuisances'.

38. *A workhouse bed* (Norfolk Museums Service: Gressenhall Museum) This bed came from Thetford Workhouse. At Gressenhall wooden beds had originally been used, but iron ones were ordered in 1836— double beds for women and single beds for men. Children under seven usually slept three to a bed. In 1853 it was reported that some children over seven did so as well, which contravened the regulations. The mattresses were filled with straw; when Harriet Kettle tried to burn down the workhouse (Source 65) she emptied the straw out of her bed and set fire to it.

On the recommendation of the visiting committee the Clerk is directed to obtain tenders for whitewashing and colouring the several wards and other apartments of the workhouse except the Board Room the walls of each to be properly sized and coloured to an extent of six feet from the floor.

39. *Minute concerning whitewashing and colouring of the workhouse* (minute book of the board of guardians of the Mitford and Launditch Union, 6 April 1874: Norfolk Record Office, C/GP14/24)

Regulations
to be observed in the Workhouse of the
Mitford and Launditch Union

	Hours of Rising	Interval for Breakfast	Time for Work	Interval for Dinner	Time for Work	Interval for Supper	Time for going to bed
From 25th March to 29th September	¼ before 6 o'clock	From½ past 6 to 7	From 7 to 12 o'clock	From 12 to 1	From 1 to 6 o'clock	From 6 to 7 o'clock	8 o'clock
From 29th September	¼ before 7 o'clock	From ½ past 7 to 8	From 8 to 12 o'clock	From 12 to 1	From 1 to 6 o'clock	From 6 to 7 o'clock	8 o'clock

These several times to be notified by ringing a Bell, and during the time of Meals, Silence, Order, and Decorum to be maintained.

40. *Regulations to be observed in the workhouse of the Mitford and Launditch Union, received by the Poor Law Board on 12 October 1851* (Public Record Office MH12 8479)

Resolved that the Master be directed to set to work all able bodied men admitted into the Workhouse (in return for the food and lodging afforded to such persons) at carting manure, Gravel or other employment suited to their respective ages, strength & capacities and that if any of such persons shall refuse or neglect to perform such task work or damage any of the property of the Board of Guardians the Master be and is hereby authorized and directed to take such person before a Magistrate in order to be dealt with according to law.

41. *Resolution concerning the employment of able bodied men in the workhouse* (minute book of the board of guardians of Mitford and Launditch Union, 12 September 1842: Norfolk Record Office, C/GP14/5) Two years after this, the guardians decided that adult able-bodied inmates should be set the task of pumping water for three and a half hours continuously. Later, oakum picking was introduced (see Source 45).

(5.)   London : KNIGHT & Co., 90, Fleet Street.   (5-69)

No. of Case.	NAME.	OFFENCE.	Date of Offence.	Punishment inflicted by Master or other Officer.
			— 1871 —	
1.	Charles Hunt (Tramp)	Refusing to pick 1lb of Oakum, in return for his nights lodging &c.	April 10	—
2.	John Wells (Tramp)	Wilfully destroying his own Clothes . viz. Coat waistcoat & Trousers	April 10	—
3.	Robert Hall (Tramp)	Wilfully destroying his own Clothes, viz. one pair of Trousers.	April 10	—
4.	Mary Ann Makins	Misbehaviour by swearing and using abusive language in the hearing of the Master, dancing on the front with another pauper instead of going to bed, and behaving in a noisy manner by shouting out of her chamber window.	May 23	Confined in a separate Room for 12 hours; and by substituting 1lb of boiled Rice in lieu of the prescribed Dietary, as ordered in Article 129.
5.	Graves Anna Maria	Disorderly conduct and misbehaviour.	June 3	—
6.	Tilch Anna	Disorderly conduct and misbehaviour, and using the following threat when brought before the Board "If no one will set fire to this nasty old place I will".	June 5	—
7.	Sullivan James (Tramp)	Wilfully breaking window of the ward in which he was then placed, and escaping from such ward to another part of the Workhouse, and other misbehaviour	Sept. 3	—
8.	Smith Thomas (Tramp)	For wilfully aiding and abetting in the above offence	Sept. 3	—

42. *Extracts from Gressenhall Workhouse Punishment Book, 1871* (Norfolk Record Office, C/GP14/105)

Opinion of Guardians thereon.	Punishment ordered by the Board of Guardians.	Date of Punishment.	Initial o Clerk.	Observations
		1871.		
—	Taken before a magistrate and committed to Swaffham prison for 1 month. h.l.	April 10	CW	
—	Taken before a magistrate and committed to Swaffham prison for 1 month. h.l.	" "	CW	
—	Taken before a magistrate and committed to Swaffham prison for 1 month. h.l.	" "	CW	
Approved by the House Com 20th May 71. CW Otherwise by the Board WDC.	—	May 24	CW	
—	To be confined 24 hours in a separate ward and diet as ordered in Article 129. —	June 6th 7th 8th 9th	CW	
—	Taken before a magistrate and committed to Wymondham Bridewell for 21 days	June 5th	CW	
—	Taken before a magistrate and committed to Swaffham prison for 21 days. h.l.	Sept. 4	CW	
—	Taken before a magistrate and committed to Swaffham prison for 21 days. h.l.	Sept. 4	CW	

The attention of the visiting committee having been called to the late communication from Mr Thornely on the subject of the allowance of beer to certain working inmates of the workhouse ... The Committee laid before the Guardians the Medical Officer's Relief Book containing the following entry—
I certify that I consider it advisable that the Paupers in the workhouse who are employed in washing, cooking, grave digging, funerals, emptying privies and drains, and in other laborious work as sanctioned by the House Committee, should be allowed extra diet of Beer, in no case exceeding two pints per head, per day, when so employed, and I beg to recommend that such allowance of Beer be granted.
Ordered that the above mentioned allowances of Beer be granted to the paupers in question.

43. *Minute concerning allowances of beer to certain working inmates of the workhouse* (minute book of the board of guardians of Mitford and Launditch Union, 21 July 1873: Norfolk Record Office, C/GP14/23)

John Craske and Ann his wife were brought before the Board to answer the complaint of the Master for stealing Bread, the ration of her own Child. Resolved that they be put into the Dungeon 24 hours each viz 12 hours at a time and that their diet be bread and water for the remainder of the week.

44. *Punishment of John and Ann Craske* (minute book of the board of guardians of Mitford and Launditch Union, 15 February 1841: Norfolk Record Office, C/GP14/4)

On the recommendation of the Visiting Committee John Walden an Inmate of the Union Workhouse and belonging to the parish of Swanton Morley is directed to be taken before a Magistrate on a charge of Misbehaviour in the Workhouse he having improperly obtained a quantity of Oakum Rope from the Workhouse Stores for the purpose of deceiving the Master as to the amount of labour performed by him as directed by the Guardians.

45. *Punishment of John Walden* (minute book of the board of guardians of Mitford and Launditch Union, 24 April 1854: Norfolk Record Office, C/GP14/11) Oakum picking as a form of employment for the 'casual' able-bodied inmates was introduced at Gressenhall in 1854. The workhouse master at the time, Mr Harrison, came from Lowestoft and was able both to buy the raw material and sell the picked oakum there. As this source suggests, oakum picking was greatly disliked by the workhouse inmates.

46. (Opposite) *Dietary for Able Bodied Paupers of Both Sexes, Mitford and Launditch Union, 1 November 1836* (Public Record Office, MH12 8477) At Gressenhall there were improvements in the diet for boys aged 10-16 in 1846, for all children aged 2-9 in 1856, and for the sick in 1868. However, it was not until the last quarter of the nineteenth century that any change took place in the diet of the able-bodied adults.

MITFORD AND LAUNDITCH UNION.

RECEIVED P.L.C.O SEP. 9 1846

TO THE GUARDIANS OF THE POOR
OF THE
MITFORD AND LAUNDITCH UNION, IN THE COUNTY OF NORFOLK;

To the Clerk or Clerks to the Justices of Petty Sessions, held for the Division or Divisions of the said County in which the Parishes and Places comprised in the said Union are situate:—and to all others whom it may concern.

We, THE POOR LAW COMMISSIONERS FOR ENGLAND AND WALES, in pursuance of the Provisions of an Act passed in the fourth and fifth Years of the Reign of His present Majesty King WILLIAM the FOURTH, intituled " *An Act for the Amendment and better Administration of the Laws relating to the Poor in England and Wales,*" do hereby order and direct that the Paupers of the respective Classes and Sexes described in the Schedule hereunto annexed, who may now or hereafter be received and maintained in the Workhouse or Workhouses of the Mitford and Launditch Union, shall, during the period of their residence therein, be fed, dieted, and maintained with the Food, and in the manner described and set forth in the said Schedule.

AND WE DO HEREBY FURTHER ORDER AND DIRECT, that every Master of the Workhouse or Workhouses of the said Union, shall cause two or more Copies of this our Order and of the said Schedule, printed in a legible manner, and in a large type, to be hung up in the most Public Places of such Workhouse or Workhouses, and to renew the same from time to time, so that it be always kept fair and legible, on pain of incurring, in case of disobedience, the Penalties provided by the aforesaid Act.

Given under our Hands and Seal, this first day of November, in the year One Thousand Eight Hundred and Thirty-six.

(Signed,)

T. FRANKLAND LEWIS.
J. G. S. LEFEVRE.
GEO. NICHOLS.

DIETARY FOR ABLE BODIED PAUPERS OF BOTH SEXES.

		BREAKFAST.		DINNER.						SUPPER.	
		Bread.	Gruel.	Suet Pudding with Vegetables.	Bread.	Cheese.	Butter.	Meat Pudding with Vegetables.	Broth.	Bread.	Cheese.
		oz.	Pints.	oz.	oz.	oz.	oz.	oz.	Pints.	oz.	oz.
SUNDAY.	Men	7	1½	-	-	-	-	14	-	7	1
	Women	6	1½	-	-	-	-	12	-	6	¾
MONDAY.	Men	7	1½	-	7	-	-	-	1½	7	1
	Women	6	1½	-	6	-	-	-	1	6	¾
TUESDAY.	Men	7	1½	-	7	1	-	-	-	7	1
	Women	6	1½	-	6	-	¾	-	-	6	¾
WEDNESDAY.	Men	7	1½	-	7	1	-	-	-	7	1
	Women	6	1½	-	6	¾	-	-	-	6	¾
THURSDAY.	Men	7	1½	14	-	-	-	-	-	7	1
	Women	6	1½	12	-	-	-	-	-	6	¾
FRIDAY.	Men	7	1½	-	7	1	-	-	-	7	1
	Women	6	1½	-	6	-	¾	-	-	6	¾
SATURDAY.	Men	7	1½	-	7	1	-	-	-	7	1
	Women	6	1½	-	6	¾	-	-	-	6	¾

OLD PEOPLE of 60 years of age and upwards, may be allowed 1 oz. of Tea, 4 oz. of Butter, and 4oz. of Sugar per Week, for those whose age and infirmities it may be deemed requisite.

CHILDREN under 9 years of age, to be dieted at discretion ; above 9 to be allowed the same quantities as Women.

SICK to be dieted as directed by the Medical Officer.

BARKER, PRINTER, DEREHAM.

47. *Names and Descriptions of Ingredients in the Diet in the Workhouse, Mitford and Launditch Union, 24 December 1849* (Public Record Office, MH12 8478)

GRESSENHALL
The inmates of the Mutford and Launditch Workhouse, 390, were bountifully supplied with roast beef, plum pudding, potatoes, ale and tobacco, on Christmas day. The women, in addition, had tea, sugar, butter and snuff; and the juvenile branches had afterwards nuts and oranges given them. The day was altogether to them one of great joy and cheerfulness. They desire to express their thanks to the Guardians for this liberal feast.

48. *Christmas Dinner at Gressenhall Workhouse* (*Norwich Mercury*, 3 January 1852) A special Christmas dinner was normally provided for the workhouse inmates, though it would appear that in the early years of the new poor law it was a privilege from which the able-bodied men and the unmarried mothers were excluded. In 1856 a group of guardians, anxious to save the ratepayers' money, succeeded in cancelling Christmas dinner completely, but it was restored the following year and continued thereafter.

ii) Guardians and officers

The board of guardians was responsible for the administration of poor relief within the poor law union which it served. The names of the guardians will be found in the minute books, and from this source it will also be possible to work out what proportion of them were regular attenders at the meetings. By checking against the lists of names in local directories, it should also be possible to analyse changes over time in the composition of the guardians in terms of occupation and social class. Disagreements among the guardians may be recorded in the form of conflicting resolutions in the minute books and it may be possible to relate these to the conflicting priorities of different occupational and social groups. Disputes between the guardians and the central authority will be evident from the MH12 correspondence, and may also be reflected in the minute books and (particularly after reporters were admitted to the guardians' meetings) the local newspapers.

The workhouse officers were appointed by the guardians and were responsible to them for the day-to-day running of the workhouse. The principal officers were the master and matron, and the porter and assistant matron. At Gressenhall in the 19th century the master and matron were invariably man and wife, but this was not always the case elsewhere. The porter and assistant matron were a married couple until 1865, but were appointed separately thereafter. Other officers included those responsible for the workhouse schools, whose numbers would vary depending on the number of children in the workhouse; and (in the case of Gressenhall) a chaplain and a medical officer, both of whom were non-resident. In the second half of the 19th century, professional nurses were also employed—previously, the guardians had relied upon inmates to carry out nursing duties.

Advertisements for officers, with details of the remuneration offered, were placed in the local press. The ease with which offices could be recruited varied from post to post, and over time. Analysis of the minute books will yield information about the extent of competition for vacancies, the background of those appointed, and the reasons for their departure. The MH12 correspondence includes completed questionnaires about new appointees.

The names of workhouse officers can be found in the registers of officers in class MH9 in the Public Record Office. They will also be discovered in the census enumerator's books for the workhouse concerned, and the name of the master at least will appear in local directories. The names and salaries of postholders may be found, more painstakingly, in the records of the quarterly salary payments in the minute books. These, and the MH12 correspondence, will yield the precise dates of appointment and resignation of officers, and may also provide details of aspects of their everyday lives, such as their diet and accommodation. There may be illustrations of the various constraints on officers; at Gressenhall, for example, they were not allowed to eat their meals in private. Testimonials, praise or reprimands by the guardians, complaints by inmates, and incidents recorded or referred to in the minute books and MH12 correspondence, may provide insights into the qualities and personalities of individual officers. From the late 19th century onwards, photographs of officers may be available, and there may be some oral testimony about those who served in the early 20th century.

Students might be asked to:

* analyse the composition of the board of guardians at various points between 1834 and
    1930, noting any significant changes
* consider evidence of disagreements among the guardians, and between them and the
    central authorities
* analyse the backgrounds of workhouse officers, and consider the motives which led
    them to become officers
* suggest why there were sometimes few applicants for the vacancies advertised by the
    guardians
* reconstruct the careers of individual officers
* identify ways in which the lives of workhouse officers were constrained
* form a judgment from the available evidence about the overall quality and conduct
    of workhouse officers

The girls lavatory is still in its objectionable state. There are 44 girls. The washhouse
which is also the lavatory is 13 ft x 11 ft and 9 ft high. The girls are all washed in
a small wooden bath which is filled and emptied by pails. The room is badly ventilated,
and the loose galvanised iron basins are fixed on no stand but placed as best they can
be.

---

49. *Extract from a report on Gressenhall Workhouse by Courtenay Boyle, assistant inspector, after his
visit on 13 February 1875* (Public Record Office, MH12 8486)

...With regard to the Girls' washhouse and bath room, the [Visiting] Committee are
of opinion, that looking to the healthy condition of the Girls under the present
arrangement, they do not feel justified in recommending any further expense on that
head.

---

50. *Extract from a letter from the clerk to the board of guardians of Mitford and Launditch Union to the
Local Government Board, 2 March 1875* (Public Record Office, MH12 8486) This source provides an
illustration of the autonomy of the guardians and the limited power of the central authority to enforce
changes in the workhouse.

Mitford and Launditch Union
MASTER AND MATRON WANTED

The Guardians of the above-named Union, will, on Monday, the 1st day of January next, at the Gressenhall Workhouse, in the county of Norfolk, proceed to elect a Married Man and his Wife, between the ages of 25 and 40 years, as MASTER and MATRON of the Gressenhall Workhouse, at the following Salaries, viz. the Master £100, the Matron £25 per annum, with Board, Washing and Lodging in the Workhouse. Qualifications and Testimonials to Character to be forwarded to the Union House, at Gressenhall, on or before the 30th day of December instant, (directed to the Clerk.) The party elected will be required to enter into a Bond, himself in £150 and two sureties in £100 each. The Candidates will be required to attend at the Gressenhall Workhouse on the day of election, and commence the duties of their situations immediately. By Order of the Board,

SAMUEL KING,
Clerk to the Union.
Litcham, 12th Dec., 1843.

---

51. *Advertisement for a master and matron, Mitford and Launditch Union* (*Norfolk Chronicle*, 23 December 1843) These vacancies were created by the departure of George Pinson and his wife Rhoda (who had been appointed in 1837 on the lower salaries of £80 and £20 per year respectively) to Norwich Castle (Source 52).

Resolved that the Board of Guardians of the Mitford and Launditch Union are unanimously of opinion that their best thanks are due to Mr and Mrs Pinson for their services as Master and Matron of Gressenhall Workhouse for nearly seven years, their kindness to the Inmates of the Workhouse has been proverbial and their great attention to the Interests of the Union by reducing the expenditure below that of any other Union very remarkable. Also their having prepared upwards of 100 orphan or deserted children for various services whereby they have been rendered useful members of Society by having been brought up in habits of cleanliness and industry and who have given very generally great satisfaction to their employers. From the great civility of Mr & Mrs Pinson at all times to the Board of Guardians they cannot help expressing their great regret at the loss of their services.

The Board also return their best thanks to Miss Pinson for the exemplary manner in which she has discharged the duties of Schoolmistress to the Gressenhall Workhouse.

---

52. *Vote of thanks to the former workhouse master and his family* (minute book of the board of guardians of Mitford and Launditch Union, 8 January 1844: Norfolk Record Office, C/GP14/6) When the assistant poor law commissioner, Sir John Walsham, heard of Mr Pinson's departure he commented: 'This is a most serious loss. I never saw any workhouse which could compare with Gressenhall Workhouse under the management of Mr and Mrs Pinson. The girls' school too under Miss Pinson's care was equally conspicuous for excellence'. Mr Pinson, master of Gressenhall Workhouse from 1837, left to become governor of the county gaol at Norwich Castle, an interesting example of a career move. The next master, George Whelan, left after two and a half years to become the governor of a lunatic asylum. The following three incumbents, Stephen Wade (1846-50), Henry Harrison (1850-58) and Robert Scraggs (1858-1868) failed to make further progress in their careers, but appear to have conducted themselves satisfactorily. Harrison was referred to by Sir John Walsham as 'an excellent officer'.

Gressenhall
July 12/71

Dear Sir

We return you our most Gratefull Thanks for your kind present of tobacco, one & all
of us, wish you every suckcess, & full & plenty, and Helth to Enjoy it. & long life,
you were kind anougf to say, that you would Remember Our Unhappy fate of being
locked up here, all Day, & hardly allowed to see the Blessed sun, through a Tyrant
like that, we hope for Humanity's sake, you will try without Injury to yourself and
Give him his Deserts. P.S. We will give you a spesiment of his caractor, He has been
Robing the pauper Inmates ever since he has been here, He has Grown Carrots and
Bete, for his poney on the land alloted to the paupers for Growing vegitables, and
likewise fed the poney on Corporation pease, and parsnips, and Bread, and potatoes,
and Gave the best of the vegitables away to his friends, He has likewise been getting
things made for himself by the Carpenter off Corporation Materials, his new Hot
House, was built off Half Corporation meterials, He took a Butifull Oak tree and Cut
it up and made two new bee hives with it, and he has been burning corporation
Fireing in his hot House, faggots, top wood, and Coal, Insted of bying it out of his
Own pockett, thereby Depriving the Inmates of their Fireing, keeping a lot of poor
Old Men perishing in the Tower with Cold, and other things too numerous to mention.
But we are lost for wants of the poore law Act. For he has Company all the week,
after Monday is over, the Visitors drop in, and they never bring any provisions with
them, they all Feast of the Corporation and you might as well be in Oxford Street
London, for the Gigs rattling all night long, to the annoyance of the sick, many a night
they have got little or no rest, and here are two Class of paupers you know, one locked
up, and the Other to lock them up. And two able men sleeping out of the House,
Dawson and Butcher, against all Laws, we should fell Glad If you would write a letter
from this, and put it in the papers, and let the Community at Large know his Rascality,
By so Doing you would oblige your old Companions The paupers of Gressenhall
Union.

53. *Letter of Complaint from the Paupers of Gressenhall Union, 12 July 1871* (Public Record Office,
MH12 8483) The next master after Robert Scraggs was Philip Reynolds (1868-93), who in this letter is
accused of peculation and of ill-treating the workhouse inmates. It was one of two letters forwarded to the
Poor Law Board by a former inmate of Gressenhall, John Webster. In a covering letter, Webster repeated
the allegations contained in the other two letters and maintained that when inmates wished to complain to
the guardians, the master locked them in. The charges were investigated by the guardians, who found them
to be without foundation. The clerk reported to the Poor Law Board that when given the opportunity to do
so, the inmates had made no complaints to the guardians, except that 'the old men were kept more closely
in their yards than before'. This, he explained, was necessitated by the major building works then in
progress. It is interesting, however, that in 1874 the guardians discovered an unexplained 'deficiency in the
stock of coals' at the workhouse, for which Reynolds was asked to pay. Further doubt about his probity (or
efficiency) is raised by evidence of failure, on occasion, to provide inmates with the correct diet (see Source
54). Reynolds resigned in January 1897 after an incumbency of almost thirty years.

The old and infirm Pauper inmates of the workhouse having complained to the Guardians of the quality of the Pea-soup and of the quality and quantity of the Tea supplied to them, the Guardians proceeded to investigate the matter of such complaints, when the Master admitted that the soup in question was improperly cooked, and that the Tea was inferior in quality. He moreover, admitted that he had supplied for 33, old and infirm Inmates 11 ounces of Tea less than the quantity prescribed by the dietary Table, and that he had erroneously entered eight quarts of Peas in the weekly provisions consumption account for the last two weeks, instead of twelve quarts the quantity actually used ...

54. *Minute concerning a complaint by the old and infirm inmates about their pea soup and tea* (minute book of the board of guardians of Mitford and Launditch Union, 28 February 1876: Norfolk Record Office, C/GP14/25)

A complaint having been made to the Guardians of the use of bad language by Thomas Butcher the Porter towards the Pauper Inmates of the workhouse and on investigation of the circumstances it appearing that such Complaint is well founded it is proposed by Mr H W Edwards and seconded by Mr Hyde that Thomas Butcher be forthwith dismissed. Amendment proposed by Mr Yaxley and seconded by Mr Rix that Thomas Butcher be reprimanded for his conduct on this and similar occasions and that such reprimand be entered on these minutes with a view to his immediate dismissal in the event of any repetition of such offence.

On taking the votes of the Guardians present and voting there appeared 3 for the original proposition and 5 for the amendment which is declared carried and Thomas Butcher is therefore called before the Board and admonished accordingly when he expressed his regret and promised not to offend again.

55. *Minute concerning a complaint against the porter* (minute book of the board of guardians of Mitford and Launditch Union, 28 March 1859: Norfolk Record Office, C/GP14/14) Porters generally stayed in post for shorter periods than the masters, although some went on to become workhouse masters themselves. Thomas Butcher escaped with a reprimand on this occasion, but four years later, 'having been represented as inattentive to and neglectful of the duties of his office', he was dismissed. Until 1865 the Mitford and Launditch guardians made joint appointments of husbands and wives as porters and assistant matrons, at a combined salary of £25 per year. Therefore when Thomas Butcher was dismissed, his wife Mary Ann, the assistant matron, had to go as well.

Lexham Hall
March 16th

Dear Sir John,

Out of the Frying Pan is an old adage, & I think likely to prove true at Gressenhall, we aimed high at your recommendation for a Schoolmistress & now are worse than we were, the last was Queen Log, this is a crazy woman without the least power over her scholars, but there was no other candidate & what was to be done. Her month is up next Monday & the board have decided upon that day to dispense with her services. We have advertized again in four County Newspapers and in the London Times. I fear our success is doubtful, the supply of the article is not equal to the demand, & like a good potation not to be procured. Perhaps it may be a dispensation, & if Lord J Russell would order another Fast we may obtain a Schoolmistress worth keeping. Our late schoolmistress is I understand elected to the Erpingham Union where no doubt she will be a treasure, if she has nothing to do. Our Field Marshall has marched off without beat of drum having traced his wife, & our boys are now no longer practising the goose step & other scientifick manoevres. We have a lot of big boys, tailors and shoemakers who really ought to be away from the house, but we do not know how to get them employed, their parishes leave them to their fate. I tell you our misfortunes, they will no doubt excite your pity, but will not help us out of our difficulties. I intended only to have told you of the fate of our Schoolmistress, but I have wandered to other subjects, & my letter will resemble and last the speech of a Member of Parliament, very little to the point, so I remain,

Yours sincerely
J W Keppel

56. Letter from Mr J W Keppel, a member (and later chairman) of the board of guardians of Mitford and Launditch Union, to Sir John Walsham, assistant poor law commissioner, 16 March 1847 (Public Record Office MH12 8478) The confiding, informal style of this letter contrasts with the icier tone of some of the more official exchanges between the guardians and the central authorities. After the departure of Harriet Pinson (see Source 52), the girls' school at Gressenhall Workhouse had a chequered career. Three incumbents came and went in quick succession, the last of these being Emily Ward, referred to as 'Queen Log' by Keppel. In January 1847, in an attempt the recruit a new and more satisfactory schoolmistress, the guardians had offered a higher salary, £25 per year instead of the £15 paid previously. This actually attracted two candidates: Mary Wardlow, who was appointed (only to be dismissed a month later) and Emily Ward, no doubt tempted to return by the increase in the salary. After the dismissal of Mary Wardlow, there was a hiatus of a month and a half before her successor, Charlotte Sparrow, took up the post. She appears to have commanded the confidence of HMI Mr Bowyer (see Source 68), but stayed for less than a year, as did the next schoolmistress.

It was not until the arrival of Charlotte Wigg (1849-1859) that stability came to the girls' school. The rapid turnover up to 1849 may help to explain why, when he visited the schools in March 1849, HMI found the girls 'inferior' to the boys (who had been taught throughout this period by one man, Robert Bradfield (Source 69). The 'Field Marshall' referred to by Keppel may have been a workhouse inmate with an army background. In September 1846 the guardians had ordered that the boys should be 'employed in the open air for two hours in each morning' and this is presumably when they practised the goose step. In September 1847, they ordered that the boys 'be drilled by Groves a pensioner in the workhouse' for an hour three afternoons a week, weather permitting. Despite these expedients, the delicate appearance of the boys was noted by HMI in 1849 (Source 69).

The Visiting Committee having this day reported to the Guardians that a dispute had arisen during the previous week between the Master and the Schoolmaster respecting a Dog which had for some months been kept on the premises by the latter without the knowledge of the Board and that the dispute in question had occasioned very improper language and behaviour between those officers more particularly on the part of the Schoolmaster, the Chairman by the desire and with the assistance of the Board investigated the circumstances of the Case and after having heard the statements of both parties he remonstrated with each upon the impropriety of his conduct and finally the matter was amicably adjusted to the satisfaction of the Guardians a stipulation being made that the Dog should be immediately sent off the premises.

57. *Minute concerning a dispute between the master and schoolmaster* (minute book of the board of guardians of Mitford and Launditch Union, 16 October 1848: Norfolk Record Office, C/GP14/8) Robert Bradfield had been appointed as workhouse schoolmaster in 1840. His youth (he was 24 at the time) and lack of training meant that the Poor Law Commissioners had had reservations about his appointment but, helped by the workhouse chaplain, he appears to have learned quickly. The boys' school was soon receiving good reports from HMI (see Sources 68 and 69). Stephen Wade, the master who was involved in this incident, was the third under whom Bradfield had worked and he may, like other workhouse schoolmasters, have found it difficult to accept the master's authority.

The question of the Schoolmaster's frequent absence from the House and his mis-apprehension of his duties having been brought before the Guardians and they having heard Mr Bradfield's explanation and again considered the purport of the letter from the Poor Law Board of 16th instant, It is agreed that the Schoolmaster's duties (amongst others) include that of seeing the Boys under his care properly to bed and in the event of his occasionally desiring to be absent from the House before the usual hour of their retiring to rest he do not delegate that duty to any of the Monitors or other Boys but consult the convenience of the Master and arrange with him to take that duty upon himself during such absence of the Schoolmaster.

58. *Minute concerning the duties of the schoolmaster* (minute book of the board of guardians of Mitford and Launditch Union, 27 July 1863: Norfolk Record Office, C/GP14/17)

On the report of the visiting committee Susan Wright is brought before the Board charged with depriving the pauper patients in the Old Men's Ward of certain Wine and other articles allowed them as Extra Medical Relief—she being then employed as Nurse in the same Ward and with having unlawfully introduced wine and spirits into the workhouse.
Ordered that Susan Wright be brought before a Magistrate to be dealt with according to law and that she be forthwith discharged from her office of Nurse.

59. *Minute concerning misconduct by the nurse* (minute book of the board of guardians of Mitford and Launditch Union, 16 December 1850: Norfolk Record Office, C/GP14/9) For these offences, Susan Wright received 14 days' imprisonment in Wymondham Bridewell. She was one of several nurses at Gressenhall in the mid-nineteenth century who were dismissed after being found wanting. Initially, nurses were recruited from among the workhouse inmates, but gradually the status of the position of superintendent nurse rose. The salary offered increased from £10 per year in 1850 to £20 per year in 1856, but recruitment remained difficult and the professional nurses who were appointed continued to be assisted by workhouse inmates. Shortly before the creation of the unified infirmary at Gressenhall in 1871, a second professional nurse was employed, but by 1897 there were still only two such posts (see Source 80).

60. *Officers and staff, Mitford and Launditch Union, c.1910* (Norfolk Museums Service: Gressenhall Museum) Seated in the centre are the master and matron, Mr and Mrs Oldman. On the extreme left is the porter, Mr Bilham (see Source 21). Some of the other men in the photograph are probably relieving officers. It is apparent that by this time the number of professional nurses had increased to four.

iii) Workhouse inmates

Statistical information about the inmates in the workhouse, and the numbers admitted and discharged week by week, may be available in the minute books or in other poor law union records. Analysis of this evidence may enable a picture to be built up of short- and long-term fluctuation in the workhouse population. Further statistics about the inmates as a whole, or about particular classes, may be found in the MH12 correspondence. Full details of the inmates (except, in some cases, their names) are available in the census returns. The registers of admissions and discharges, where they exist, will contain the names of those involved. At Gressenhall, some inmates' names can be found scratched on the wall which surrounded one of the exercise yards, and these can be linked with references in the documentary sources.

The treatment of particular classes of inmates could be investigated in detail. Poor law inspectors' reports, filed with the MH12 correspondence, always included reference to provision in the workhouse for the sick and vagrants. The vagrants, or 'casual poor', were a class apart, both physically and in relation to their treatment in the workhouse. It may be possible to identify accommodation for vagrants on site, and to collect further details of their treatment from material in the MH12 correspondence, the minute books, and other sources such as parliamentary papers.

Similar evidence may be found about single women with children. Guardians were expected, where possible and appropriate, to subdivide classes according to the 'moral character or behaviour or previous habits' of the inmates. Single women with children were often kept apart from other inmates and subjected to a particularly harsh regime.

Material could also be collected about the treatment of the sick and handicapped. The infirmary accommodation may be identifiable, and the documentary sources will contain references to the conditions there. Reports by visiting 'commissioners in lunacy' will be filed with the MH12 correspondence and will be referred to in the poor law inspectors' reports.

References to individual inmates by name occur frequently in the minute books, and may also be found in other poor law union records and in the MH12 correspondence. Occasionally, detailed information may be discovered about an individual. Even more rarely, letters of complaint by inmates may be found in the MH12 correspondence (see source 53). By collating all of the available material, it may be possible to build up life histories of individuals.

Students might be asked to:

* consider the range of circumstances which led people to become workhouse inmates
* compare the treatment received by different groups of inmates, and make a judgment about whether the differences in the treatment given were appropriate
* reconstruct as far as the sources allow the life history of an individual workhouse inmate
* consider why some inmates complained or protested, but the majority did not

COUNTY and UNION	Regulations in force in the Union as to the Reception and Relief of Casual Poor in the Workhouse 1.	Hour of Admission 2.	Amount and Nature of Food given 3.	Work exacted in Return 4
NORFOLK Depwade	The master of the workhouse sets every adult person not suffering under any temporary or permanent infirmity of body, being an occasional poor person who shall be relieved in the workhouse, in return for the food and lodging afforded to such person, to perform the following task of work, that is to say: such person shall pick 1lb. of oakum, provided that no such person shall be detained against his or her will for the performance of such task of work for any time exceeding four hours from the hour of breakfast the next morning after admission; and provided also that such amount of work shall not be required from any person to whose age, strength and capacity it shall appear not to be suited.	No specified hour	Men, 7 oz. of bread and 1½ pint of gruel for breakfast and supper; women, 5oz. of bread and 1 pint of gruel for breakfast and supper.	Picking 1lb. of oakum
Loddon and Clavering	Upon the admission of casual poor, they are cleansed by means of a warm bath, and placed in wards set apart and kept for their reception; male and female.	After 6 p.m.; or at any hour day or night, in case of sickness.	6 oz. of bread, with 1 oz. of cheese for supper; 7 oz. of bread, with 1 oz. of cheese for break-fast.	To pick 1lb. of oakum rope
Mitford and Launditch	They are admitted for one night by order of a relieving officer or overseer; and five police officers resident in certain parishes are also appointed assistant relieving officers, and give orders in like manner to this class of poor only.	At all times	Supper, 7 oz. of bread and 1 oz. of cheese; breakfast, 7 oz. of bread and 1½ pints of gruel.	1 lb. of oakum to be picked by each male person of 16 years old and upwards.

61. *Extracts from Returns relating to the Casual Poor in Workhouses* (Parliamentary Papers, 1864)

Milford & Launditch Union.

REGD
P L.B.
APR 10
1861

A RETURN of all FEMALE PAUPERS of the Age of 16 years and upwards in the Workhouse on the *sixth* day of ~~March~~ *April* 1861, classified according to character.

		TOTAL.
1.	Single women pregnant with their first child - - -	1
2.	Single women who have had one bastard child - - -	5
3.	Single women who have had one bastard child and are pregnant again - - - - - - - - -	4
4.	Single women who have had two bastard children - - -	5
5.	Single women who have had three bastard children - -	3
6.	Single women who have had four or more bastard children -	3
7.	Idiotic or weak-minded single women with one or more bastard children - - - - - - - -	,,
8.	Women whose out-relief has been taken off on account of misconduct	,,
9.	Women incapable of getting their own living from syphilis -	,,
10.	Prostitutes - - - - - - - - -	,,
11.	Girls who have been out at service, but do not keep their places on account of misconduct - - - - -	1
12.	Girls brought up in the Workhouse and who have been out at service, but have returned on account of misconduct - -	3
13.	Widows who have had one or more bastard children during their widowhood - - - - - - - -	4
14.	Married women with husbands in the Workhouse - -	4
15.	Married women with husbands transported or in gaol - -	,,
16.	Married women deserted by their husbands - - -	3
17.	Imbecile, idiotic, or weak-minded women and girls - -	7
18.	Respectable women and girls incapable of getting their living on account of illness or other bodily defect or infirmity - -	7
19.	Respectable able-bodied women and girls - - -	6
20.	Respectable aged women - - - - -	7
		63.

I certify the above return as correct,

R. W. Scraggs

Master of the Workhouse.

2226.   E. & S.—750.—3/61.

5 April 1861

62. *Return of Female Paupers in the Workhouse, Classified according to Character: Mitford and Launditch Union, 6 April 1861* (Public Record Office, MH32 84)

Distinguishing dress for
Workhouse Inmates

Sir,

In my recent inspection of the Gressenhall Workhouse a complaint was addressed to me by a female inmate—a married woman—and afterwards by her husband, also an inmate—which involved one or two peculiarities.

It is the custom in this large Workhouse, as in many others in my district, to sub-classify the able-bodied women, and it is also generally but not peremptorily the custom to place the married women in one ward and the single women with illegitimate children in the other ward.

Some time—about a year ago—the woman who appealed to me against being any longer classed among what both she, and subsequently her husband contemptuously termed "the Jacket women" (an expression which I will shortly explain), left the Workhouse with a one legged man, likewise a pauper but younger than herself, and eventually married him—shortly after which both returned to the Workhouse, the woman pregnant, and have remained there ever since.

On returning, the woman backed by her husband demanded as of right that she should no longer be placed in her old ward where (*having three bastard children*) she had heretofore been placed, but with the married women, as being now a married woman. Looking to her antecedents and to the objectionableness of two pauper inmates leaving the Workhouse—living for a time in a state of concubinage (*It is right to remark that the woman denies this, though the Guardians entertain no doubt of the fact) —then marrying—and almost immediately returning to the Workhouse to be maintained there at the expense of the ratepayers—looking to these circumstances the Guardians considered the claim set up preposterous. Nevertheless they consulted me on the point and I ruled that under Article 99 secondly of the Consolidated Order, they were fully competent to direct the Master to place her in her old ward notwithstanding her being now a married woman. I repeated this to the woman herself but as she alleged that other women with illegitimate children born before marriage, had after marriage been transferred from the single women's to the married women's ward, and that it was hard to have old transgressions always hung as it were round her neck, I have requested the Guardians to reconsider the question on the special ground (supposing it to be sustainable by facts) that a different measure has been dealt out to her than to other women similarly circumstanced. The principal point, however, to which I wish to attract the Board's attention is this:—The dresses of the married and single women are so exactly alike as to materials that I was myself quite unconscious of any difference—but it appears that for many years the Guardians have required the single women to wear a distinguishing overdress or *Jacket*, of the same materials as the gown, coming down to the hips. Hence the expression, *used and felt as a term of reproach*, of "Jacket women".

Now adverting to the note (u) at page 84 of Glen's Poor Board Orders, it is evident—indeed the Master fully admitted such to be the case—that the women consider this distinguishing overdress, limited as it is to the women of unchaste behaviour, to be a mark of disgrace.

Can the Guardians properly enforce its continuance, however unobjectionable it may be in appearance?

I have the honour to be,
Sir,
Your obedient servant,
John Walsham.

63. (Opposite) *Letter from Sir John Walsham, poor law inspector, to the Poor Law Board, concerning distinguishing dress for workhouse inmates, 24 September 1866* (Public Record Office, MH12 8482) Article 99, 'secondly', cited by Sir John Walsham, refers to the subdivision of classes in the workhouse, 'with reference to the moral character or behaviour or the previous habits of the inmates'. Thus the justification for placing the woman in this case in the 'jacketers' ward' would have been in terms of her previous habits. As a result of Sir John Walsham's intervention, the guardians immediately abolished the use of the 'jacket' at Gressenhall, but use of the term 'jacketer' appears to have continued for some time (see Source 84).

There are at present 18 inmates (11 of the male and 7 of the female sex) who are classed as of unsound mind at this workhouse, and I have added to the list a man named John Jarrett, and a woman named Peace Pratt, to whose cases my attention was drawn by the Master. Both are decidely imbecile. The latter has had two illegitimate children before she came into the house and is evidently unable to take care of herself. As she has no settled home she ought not to be allowed to leave the workhouse.

The whole of these patients appear to be chronic and harmless, are reported to be easily managed in association with the ordinary inmates, and a fair number are usefully employed. The clothes of several of the men needed change and repair, but otherwise the personal condition of both sexes was, upon the whole, satisfactory. Although my visit was made before 9 a.m. and when the beds in the sick wards were all occupied, there was nothing offensive or impure in the atmosphere of the rooms, owing to the ample cubical space afforded to each person.

The beds were clean and well filled, but they are throughout of straw.

For the aged, the infirm and the bedridden I recommend that flock or some other soft material be substituted.

I have satisfaction in reporting an improvement since the last visit in the dietary of the insane inmates. All have now better food than the able bodied paupers.

Twelve of the number have meat dinners daily; they have all bread and milk for breakfast, and tea with bread and butter for supper. Four of each sex have also wine, spirits or porter daily.

64. (Above) *A report on Gressenhall Workhouse by Mr Cleaton, commissioner in lunacy, following his visit on 25 November 1869* (Public Record Office, MH12 8483)

Mitford and Launditch Union
Monday, Charles Wright, Clerk.
East Dereham
17th July 1865

My Lords and Gentlemen,

Harriet Kettle. Out relief.

Harriet Kettle, a single woman, had previously to November 1858 been from time to time a Pauper inmate of the Mitford and Launditch Union Workhouse, wherein her ungovernable temper and disorderly conduct occasioned her to be frequently punished, not only under the rules of the Poor Law Board as a refractory Pauper, but also under the provisions of 55 Geo.3 and the 7th to 8th Vic. and the records of her punishment show that for such offences she was convicted before the Magistrates and sentenced as follows.

On 13th September 1852 for 14 days
" 3rd November 1852 for 21 days
" 10th January 1853 for 42 days
" 21st September 1855 for 42 days
" 21st January 1856 for 21 days

During her confinement on the last of these occasions in Little Walsingham Prison her conduct became so violent that she was deemed by the Medical Officer of the Prison to be insane and the requisite measures were taken for her removal to the County Lunatic Asylum at Thorpe, where however she remained but a short period, after which she returned again to the Union Workhouse, discharged as sane. On the 20th of November 1858 she attempted to set fire to the Workhouse and was accordingly committed on that charge for trial at the then ensuing Lent Assizes for this County. While awaiting her trial, in custody in the House of Correction at Wymondham, she was again by reason of her violent conduct, thought to be insane, and was in like manner as before removed to the Thorpe Asylum and did not, therefore, appear to take her trial at those Assizes, although a true bill was returned against her for the offence in question.

Having been received into the Asylum under an order from the Secretary of State in accordance with the terms of the statute she of course remained in the Lunatic Asylum for a short period for the purpose (it is assumed) of testing her sanity, but the medical officers of that Institution never deemed her insane, at any time; and accordingly, at the Summer Assizes of 1859 she was brought into Court for the purpose of arraignment, when her violent language and manner towards the Court and others caused her to be sent back to the Asylum and it was not until the Lent Assizes in March 1860, that she was arraigned on the before mentioned Indictment. Upon that occasion she again repeated her violent abusive and indecent language before Mr Justice Williams, who after hearing the history of her previous conduct and the evidence of Mr Owen the Governor of the Lunatic Asylum, allowed the trial to proceed and she was ultimately tried, convicted and sentenced to 18 Calendar months imprisonment in Wymondham House of Correction the Prison from which she had been previously removed to the Asylum.

Soon after her return into the Custody of the Matron of the Wymondham House of Correction she was again certified to be insane, and on the 20th of the following April she was by order of Sir George Cornewall Lewis, again sent to the Thorpe Asylum where she remained until August 1861 when in consequence of her insanity she was removed as a Criminal Lunatic to St George's in the fields where she continued a prisoner until 18th of October 1861, when she was discharged as sane at the expiration of her sentence.

Since her return she has been from time to time allowed outdoor relief (as sanctioned by your letter of the 14th of November 1861) and having recently exhibited symptoms of Phthisis, a small allowance has been continued to her during her residence as a single woman in the Parish of East Dereham, the cost of such relief being then, under the provisions of the late statutes, charged to the Common Fund of the Union. Within the last month or thereabouts Harriet Kettle has been married to one [blank] Head an agricultural labourer belonging to the parish of East Dereham, but as he is for the remainder of the current year, up to Old Michaelmas next under a contract of service as team-man to his Master, with whom he resides, and as he has no weekly wages nor other means to maintain his wife or to provide her with a home, the Guardians, having regard to her antecedents, and to her present state of Mental and Bodily Health, deem it advisable to continue her outdoor relief until her husband is in a position to contribute to her maintenance. The Guardians and Parish Officers of East Dereham to which she is now chargeable are dissatisfied with this arrangement, and I am, therefore, directed to bring the matter again under your notice and to enquire whether the Guardians are justified in the course they have adopted.

I enclose the Medical Officer's last certificate for your perusal.

And have the honor to be,
My lords and gentlemen,
Your most obed[ien]t serv[an]t
Charles Wright

[enclosure]

Harriet Head age 26 of East Dereham has for some time past suffered from symptoms of Phthisis, and she is never free from cough and frequently has attacks of Haemophysis (a spitting of blood). It is true that the lung disorganisation progresses slowly but consumption is frequently a malady of very slow progress. Her general health, I think, is somewhat improved since she left the Lunatic Asylum at Thorpe but I do not consider her state of mind at all improved, and altho' she is hardly a fit subject for confinement in an Asylum, yet, she may be said to suffer from what I sh[oul]d call *Moral Insanity* a term according—to Forbes Winslow used to designate a form of disease in which the sentiments, affections, habits and the moral feeling of the mind rather than the intellectual faculties are in an unsound and disordered state. I am of opinion that her removal to the Union workhouse would prove injurious in a medical point of view: at all events, aggravate or be likely to aggravate, the form of mental disease for the treatment of which she has already been twice sent to asylums.

H.C.Hastings
Med[ical] Off[icer]

East Dereham
July 15 1865

65. *Letter from the clerk to the board of guardians of Mitford and Launditch Union to the Poor Law Board, concerning Harriet Kettle, 17 July 1865* (Public Record Office, MH12 8482) A great deal of information about Harriet Kettle, a workhouse inmate, can be discovered from the guardians' minute book and a range of other sources. In 1863 the medical officer of the County Lunatic Asylum described her as follows: 'She is very short, and small, neat and tidy in her person, quick and intelligent, and with a great deal of self possession. Her features are somewhat coarse, the lips thick, and her face has a repulsive look, showing cunning, low breeding, the sort of defiance resulting from her long continued and well known wickedness ... She blames the world for some of her follies, and says she could not earn a living honestly, not being strong enough for service'. Despite the doubtful state of her health in 1865, the census returns of 1871 show Harriet Kettle/Head living with her husband and their two children in Dereham. By 1881 they had moved house and had four children, and by 1891 Harriet was a grandmother.

66. *A group of inmates, Gressenhall Workhouse, pre-1914* (Norfolk Museums Service: Gressenhall Museum)

iv) Children

Investigation of the theme of children in the workhouse may prove to be of particular interest for students. Inevitably, account will need to be taken of the received stereotype represented by Oliver Twist, and investigation might usefully focus on the extent to which the reality matched this stereotype.

As for other groups of inmates, information about children in the workhouse may be obtained from census returns, references in the minute books and MH12 correspondence, and a variety of other sources. Oral testimony about workhouse conditions in the early twentieth century, when it can be obtained, is almost inevitably going to relate the experience of those who were workhouse inmates as children.

The sources will provide evidence about how children were affected by the regulations and routines of the workhouse and the extent to which efforts were made to improve their health and welfare. The education, training and employment of workhouse children are topics which exercised both the guardians and the central authorities, and there may be much material about them in the minute books and MH12 correspondence. The reports of visiting poor law inspectors, in MH12, always include a comment on the workhouse school, and those of H.M. Inspectors of Schools are often reproduced in full.

Students might be asked to:
* identify any respects in which children were treated better than other inmates
* identify other respects in which the treatment of children was harsh
* explain why some children subsequently expressed gratitude for their treatment
* assess the extent to which the treatment of children matched that of Oliver Twist as described by Dickens

Mitford and Launditch UNION.

TABLE, shewing the number, &c., of Children in the Workhouse of the *Mitford and Launditch* — Union, on Thursday the Eighteenth day of March, 1847.

CHILDREN IN THE WORKHOUSE	BOYS				GIRLS			
	Under 3 years Old	3 years Old and under 7	7 years Old and upwards	TOTALS	Under 3 years Old	3 years Old and under 7	7 years Old and upwards	TOTALS
Illegitimate,—their Mothers in the Workhouse..........	6	8	4	18	7	4	6	17
Illegitimate,—their Mothers not in the Workhouse.........	1	1	3	5	1	-	2	3
Children of Widows who are in the Workhouse..........	1	4	4	9	1	-	3	4
Children of Widows who are not in the Workhouse	-	2	4	6	-	-	5	5
Children of Widowers who are in the Workhouse.........	-	1	1	2	-	1	2	3
Children of Widowers who are not in the Workhouse	-	-	-	-	-	-	-	-
Children whose Father and Mother are dead	2	4	23	29	-	5	23	28
Children deserted by Father....	-	-	7	7	3	4	10	17
Children deserted by Mother...	-	1	2	3	-	-	3	3
Children deserted by both Parents	-	-	1	1	-	-	1	1
Children whose Father is transported, or suffering imprisonment for crime	2	-	-	2	1	-	-	1
Children whose residence in the Workhouse is caused by the bodily or mental infirmity of their Father or Mother ...	-	-	1	1	2	2	2	6
Children of able-bodied Parents who are in the Workhouse .	4	1	6	11	3	5	7	15
Children of able-bodied Parents who are not in the Workhouse..............	-	-	1	1	-	-	-	-
Children not falling within any of the foregoing Classes ..	-	2	1	3	-	-	2	2
TOTALS....	16	24	58	98	18	21	66	105

NOTE.—No Child is to be enumerated more than once, though such Child might fall within more than one Class.

Summary of Children in the Workhouse.

Boys.......... 98
Girls.......... 105
TOTAL.. 203

Signed this 31st day of *March* 1847.

Clerk to the Guardians.

67. *Table concerning Children in the Workhouse, Mitford and Launditch Union, sent to the Poor Law Board, 31 March 1847* (Public Record Office, MH12 8478)

The Master reported that Her Majesty's Inspector of Schools had visited the Workhouse on Thursday last and the following report as entered in the Visitors' Book was laid before the Board.

November 4th
1847

I may say that I was not only satisfied but surprised at the quickness and intelligence evinced by the Boys in their answers upon Scripture and their general proficiency which far surpasses that I have hitherto witnessed in the County. The Girls are more backward but I have no doubt that their present Mistress will soon raise them to the level of the boys. The only suggestions I think it necessary to make for the purpose of further increasing the efficiency of the School are First. To furnish both boys and girls with a sufficient number of secular Books conveying useful and entertaining information. The best that I know are those published for the use of Schools by the Irish Commission for National Education. I also recommend Dr Davies's History of England, a set of penny magazines and Saturday magazines would also form an useful little library to occupy the leisure hours of the boys. The second thing I would recommend is an alteration in the arrangement of the Desks at present they are ranged along the Walls a Disposition now abandoned in the best National Schools as affording no facilities for simultaneous instruction. Parallel Desks are now being generally adopted and have been everywhere strongly recommended by Her Majesty's Inspectors of National Schools especially the Reverend Mr Cook and the Reverend H Mosely who has given in his report for 1846 the exact dimensions of those used in the National Society's training School at Battersea. A Copy of Tales Arithmetic and Sullivans Geography generalised would also be a great help to the Master.
Signed

H G Bowyer
H M Inspr of Schools

In compliance with Mr Bowyer's recommendation the clerk is directed to procure for the workhouse schools two vols of Dr Davies's History of England two vols of Tales' Arithmetic and two vols of Sullivans Geography Generalized.

68. (Above) *Minute concerning a report by HMI Mr H G Bowyer, on the schools at Gressenhall Workhouse, following his visit on 4 November 1847* (minute book of the board of guardians of Mitford and Launditch Union, 8 November 1847: Norfolk Record Office, C/GP14/8)

69. (Opposite) *A report on the schools at Gressenhall Workhouse by HMI Mr H G Bowyer, following his visit in March 1849* (Public Record Office, MH12 8478) As in 1847 (see Source 68) Mr Bowyer's observations were heeded by the guardians. Two boys were appointed as pupil teachers—one of them was eventually appointed to the position of schoolmaster in another workhouse. An infant schoolmistress was appointed in July 1850. Agricultural training for the boys was provided on an 'industrial farm' established on land near the workhouse buildings. In 1853 the guardians reported that 'the improved physical condition of the boys is manifest', and announced their intention of buying two cows so that girls could be trained in dairy work. The vocational training of the girls, however, was largely in other skills: they were taught needlework and knitting, and some were employed in the laundry under the supervision of one of the adult female inmates. HMI's greater concern with the boys than with the girls is evident in both this source and Source 68.

March 1849

I have this day inspected the Schools. They boys answered remarkably well in the Scriptures. Indeed their religious knowledge would do credit to any school.

Their Arithmetic is very fair; and they possess greater knowledge of Geography than is usually the case in schools of [this] description. I however think that more attention has perhaps been bestowed on the higher and more showy branches of knowledge than in the humbler but essential ones, of reading and writing. Their reading, though certainly better than it was at my last visit is still much below their other attainments, and inferior to that in many schools of humbler pretensions.

Their writing, though certainly fair, might be improved; and they are imperfect in writing from dictation which is a great defect in a School.

I hope, however that, by devoting more time to these things the defects I have mentioned will be speedily corrected.

I must, however, say that it is impossible for one man, unassisted by permanent monitors, to attend properly to a school of 80 boys: and most of the deficiencies of the lower Classes evidently proceed from this cause. I would strongly recommend to the Board to allow 2 or 3 of the more promising boys to be trained as Pupil Teachers, as it will not only greatly improve the school but open to those boys a new sphere of usefulness as Schoolmasters.

I also wish to submit to the consideration of the Board the expediency of providing some industrial training for the boys, besides shoemaking, and tailoring: as these trades are neither calculated to enable them to earn a subsistence, nor to render them sufficiently vigourous to perform the duties of an agricultural labourer. The appearance of the boys clearly shows that they have been too delicately brought up. They have not the vigourous and healthy countenances of rustic lads, but the white and delicate faces of girls; and it is evident they are not calculated to support the laborious life to which they are destined.

This might easily be remedied by adopting the system of agricultural training which has been found go successful, in the Farm School establishment in the Bridgnorth Union, and which is now introduced at the Wortham Workhouse. By keeping a few cows, the girls might also be instructed in the business of the dairy, which would greatly increase their chance of finding employment.

An agricultural school of this description would not be expensive; but profitable to the Union, as it would employ labour which is now maintained in comparative idleness. The produce of the land cultivated on the most approved principles of spadehusbandry, has been found in several workhouses to exceed considerably that of ordinary farming. At the Bedford and Guiltcross Union Workhouses, in the former of which only the ablebodied men are employed on the land, the net profit averages £17 per acre: and if cows were kept it would, I am confident, be much greater. The Board would also find that it would be much easier to procure places for the boys and girls thus trained to their future duties than it is at present and that the children would also turn out much better.

There are about 30 infants who receive, at present, no other instruction than that which can be afforded by the pauper women of the house; and they consequently come into the other Schools knowing hardly anything. So large a number of infants would form a good Infant School, and I would recommend that an Infant Schoolmistress should be procured for them.

H. G. Bowyer
H. M. Inspector of Schools

I found the girls inferior to the boys in every respect.

From a statement prepared by Robert Bradfield the Union schoolmaster and this day laid before the Board it appeared that since the year 1845 and up to the present time 88 Boys had left the Workhouse School and gone into service in the several capacities and employments as follows vizt.:

Artists	1	Printers	1
Army	8	Shoemakers	5
Carpenters	2	Tailors	4
Gentlemen's Service	11	Schoolmasters	4
Harness maker	1	Farm Service	12
Not known	12	Other employments	26

70. *Minute concerning destinations of boys leaving the workhouse school* (minute book of the board of guardians of Mitford and Launditch Union, 11 July 1853: Norfolk Record Office, C/GP14/11)

Benjamin Howlett of Oxwick aged 15 years and Thomas Eke of Southbergh aged 14 years two inmates of the union workhouse, were brought before the Board charged with absconding from the workhouse on Tuesday last. It being Howlett's first offence and as he appeared to regret it and promised not to do so again he was admonished by the Board in the presence of the Schoolmaster and cautioned as to his future behaviour, but Eke having before absconded was ordered to be kept in a separate dark room for 48 hours with bread and water diet.

71. *Punishment of Benjamin Howlett and Thomas Eke* (minute book of the board of guardians of Mitford and Launditch Union, 8 August 1870: Norfolk Record Office, C/GP14/21) This is probably the Thomas Eke referred to in Sources 83 and 84.

The Visiting Committee having called the attention of the Guardians to the unhealthy state of the boys' eyes as compared with those of the girls in the union schools and having suggested that an improvement might possibly be effected by more frequent exercise in the open air. It is agreed that on such recommendation Mr Bradfield be directed to take the boys out for a walk with him (weather permitting) three days in the week besides Sunday for not less than one hour on each occasion and one of such walks being at the hour of eleven in the forenoon. And further that the Master of the Workhouse be empowered at his discretion to make arrangements with Mr Bradfield for providing similar recreation for the boys on each Sunday by walking into the country and occasional attendance at the parish church when practicable and convenient.

72. *Minute concerning exercise for the boys in the workhouse* (minute book of the board of guardians of Mitford and Launditch Union, 6 June 1864: Norfolk Record Office, C/GP14/17) Ophthalmia was a common complaint among children in workhouses. In the 1860s the visiting committee of the board of guardians manifested considerable concern about the health of the younger boys who were not employed on the 'industrial farm'. In the summer of 1865, the master was instructed to take the boys swimming in the local river, 'in such place ... as he in his discretion may find most suitable for the purpose and unobjectionable to the public'.

Mr George Wombwell having on Friday last gratuitously admitted all the children of the workhouse schools to his exhibition of wild beasts at East Dereham the Clerk is ordered to convey to Mr Wombwell the Guardians' sense of his kindness on this occasion.

73. *Minute concerning Mr Wombwell's exhibition of wild beasts* (minute book of the board of guardians of Mitford and Launditch Union, 3 March 1851: Norfolk Record Office, C/GP14/10)

On the recommendation of the Visiting Committee, leave is given to the Mistresses of the workhouse schools to take such of the girls belonging to those schools as they and the Master and Matron may deem proper, for an excursion to the seaside on Thursday next, the necessary pecuniary means having been provided for this purpose.

74. *Minute concerning an excursion to the seaside* (minute book of the board of guardians of Mitford and Launditch Union, 7 July 1862: Norfolk Record Office, C/GP14/16)

Mr John Porter Smith called the attention of the Guardians to the circumstance of the intended passage of the Prince and Princess of Wales through the town of Dereham on Monday next and on Mr Smith's proposition the children of the Workhouse Schools are to be allowed to witness the procession if the weather permit.

75. *Minute concerning the visit of the Prince and Princess of Wales to Dereham* (minute book of the board of guardians of Mitford and Launditch Union, 27 November 1865: Norfolk Record Office, C/GP14/18)

The clerk laid before the Board a letter dated the 9th of May last from William B. Pye now residing at Chicago in North America expressive of his gratitude to the Guardians for the education, care and kindness received by him as a child when a pauper inmate of this workhouse.

76. *Minute concerning a letter from William B. Pye of Chicago* (minute book of the board of guardians of Mitford and Launditch Union, 1 June 1863 (Norfolk Record Office, C/GP14/17)

—What happened to you after your father died?

—Me and a brother of mine and a sister—my mother ... couldn't maintain us and the man who come and visit the people and give them some money if they in want, but he would not give her any help and so my mother said, "Well, I'll make you keep some of them". And so she took us three to the workhouse.

—How old were you when you went there?

—Six year old. My sister was about nine and my brother he must have been twelve.

—Did you go in the daytime or at night?

—In the daytime, and my sister howled because they took her out of the bathroom first and me and my brother went in the bath, we had a bath and they put all clean clothes on us. Corduroy suits they were. They were inclined to be brown. Corduroy suits. Didn't my sister cry. When we got up at our tea table she said, "I want my brother Willie". That's how she went on all that night when we were getting our teas.

—Do you remember the food?

—Oh yes. Breakfast we had porridge, porridge and bread and a piece of butter on it. That was breakfast, porridge, a basin of porridge.

—What did you have for lunch?

—Oh we didn't have too bad a living. Beef, potatoes, sometimes bacon, sometimes pie. Oh I can't grumble about the meals at all. Can't grumble at all.

—Did you have any tea or supper?

—We never had any supper, we had tea at six o'clock at night ... But the latter part of the time I was in there they sent us boys to Gressenhall school. You know where that is, up near where the parson lives. They sent us boys to Gressenhall school. And they fitted us out with a civilian suit ...

—Can you remember the school room ... in the workhouse?

—Well, it looked just like an ordinary school. We had a governess, a very nice person. She got married to an inmate. That's an uncommon thing to do, isn't it? She was a nice woman, governess, she married an inmate. Well, the girls, they didn't go out to school. We used to walk to Gressenhall [village] school when we packed up the union [ie, when the boys' school at the workhouse was closed] ... Well one day I went to Gressenhall with the other boys and they kept jeering at us because we were workhouse boys. Well, I said to my boy friends, I said: "I'll pay him out for jeering at us". I said: "We're a lot better off than him". I said: "We've got better clothes and better grub than he has". And so when he came out here I laid him out for dead. We all went away and left him laying on the ground and when I got back to Gressenhall there wasn't a word said about it. But the boy's mother—he was a six foot boy and I ... wasn't no more than five feet, that's for sure—had given him up for dead, so I must have sold him a proper one, mustn't I?

—How did they heat the schoolroom [in the workhouse]?

—[They had] what you call a tortoiseshell stove ... Burn about a hundredweight of coal a week, well might be more, depend on the weather. We didn't want a fire not in the summer time, but we did want one in the winter, because we never had nothing to do. Although we got plenty of exercise because we had a big yard to play in. That was always locked, you know. Yes, where we stayed in and played, that was always locked. But when we went out to meal times the bell used to ring up top, close to where the clock is ...

77. *Oral testimony of a former inmate of Gressenhall Workhouse* (Norfolk Museums Service: Gressenhall Museum) He was born in 1884 and was admitted to the workhouse in 1890. The tape recording was made in 1976, when he was 92.

78. *Children at Gressenhall school, pre-1912* (Norfolk Museums Service: Gressenhall Museum) Towards the end of the 19th century the number of children in the workhouse declined, and the guardians considered sending them to local schools rather than themselves employing schoolmasters and schoolmistresses. The children attended Gressenhall village school from October 1884, but their presence does not appear to have been greatly welcomed, and in 1887 they were withdrawn. From 1898 onwards, the workhouse boys were again sent to Gressenhall village school, while the girls were sent to the school in the adjoining parish of Beetley. In this photograph, the workhouse boys can be identified by their shaven heads. As source 77 suggests, they were sometimes taunted by the other children.

v) Workhouse life at the turn of the century

The focus of this theme will be on the extent and nature of continuity and change in the union workhouse up to about 1900. By the end of the 19th century, there had been several changes in workhouse life. Some of them were accompanied by changes in the buildings—for example, in the case of Gressenhall, the creation of a separate infirmary and the provision of central heating and a proper system of drainage. Others involved the selective revision of some of the harsher regulations, for some at least of the workhouse inmates. In other respects, however, it may be the continuity of the workhouse experience which is more apparent.

To investigate workhouse life at the turn of the century use can be made of the same sources as those relating to earlier periods, supplemented by certain new sources—for example, photographs and newspaper reports of guardians' meetings.

Students might be asked to:

* identify ways in which life had improved for workhouse inmates by the end of the
    19th century
* identify ways in which it had not improved
* assess the extent to which there had been changes in the attitudes of guardians,
    officers and inmates
* assess the overall significance of the changes which had taken place

---

December 14 ... To-day I went with a friend, who is one of the guardians of the poor for this district, to visit Heckingham Workhouse, where I have not been for about fourteen years. Once I was a guardian there myself, and in that capacity used to sit upon the Board, but after a year or two's experience of it I resigned the office, which I confess I did not find congenial. There are few things more depressing than to listen, fortnight by fortnight, to the tales of utter poverty and woe poured out by the applicants for relief from the rates ... It astonished me to see how greatly the conditions of existence at Heckingham have been improved of late years. Now it resembles an infirmary for the aged poor, rather than the last shelter to which the destitute are driven by necessity. In the old days, indeed, it was a dreary place; for instance, I remember the sick ward, a cold and desolate room, where two children, to whom I used to carry toys, a twin brother and sister, lay dreadfully ill of some scrofulous disease, with no fire in the grate, and, so far as I recollect, no trained nurse to wait upon them. To-day that ward is bright and cheerful, with a good fire burning in it and a properly certificated attendant to minister to the wants of its occupants ...

In truth, to whatever extent it may be brightened and rendered habitable, one cannot pretend that a workhouse is a cheerful place. The poor girls, with their illegitimate children creeping, dirty-faced, across the floor of brick; the old, old women lying in bed too feeble to move, or crouching round the fire in their mob-caps, some of them stern-faced with much gazing down the dim vista of the past, peopled for them with dead, with much brooding on the present and the lot which it has brought them; others vacuous and smiling—'a little gone', the master whispers; others quite childish and full of complaints; all of these are no more cheerful to look on than is the dull appropriate light of this December afternoon. The old men, too, their hands knobbed and knotted with decades of hard work, their backs bent, their faces often almost grotesque, like those caricatures of humanity we see carved upon the handle of a stick, come here at last in reward of their labours—well, as the French writer says, 'cela donne furieusement a penser'. It is not the place that is so melancholy, it is this poignant example of the sad end of life and all its toilings; it is the forlorn, half-dazed aspect of these battered human hulks who once were young, and strong, and comely ...

79. *Heckingham Workhouse*, from H. Rider Haggard, *A Farmer's Year* (1899)

WORKHOUSE ADMINISTRATION AT GRESSENHALL
CONDEMNATORY SPEECH BY HER MAJESTY'S INSPECTOR

The fortnightly meeting of the members of this Board was held at the Workhouse, Gressenhall, on Monday, the CHAIRMAN (MR T H HUBBARD presiding. Mr T H Bagenal (Her Majesty's Poor Law Inspector of the District) was also present ...

At the conclusion of the business ... MR BAGENAL rose, addressed the Board upon the observations he had made in connection with two visits he had recently made to the Workhouse ... The Inspector said that he should have paid them a visit before, but that his district was a very large one, and it took him a considerable time to get round. He was particularly glad to be there that day because of the discussions which had taken place in respect to the building alterations...It appeared they had not taken in hand any new work they were morally bound to do by their correspondence with the Board, because they were not satisfied with the work in hand. He was not very much surprised at it. The moral of the whole thing was that when they undertook to get the work of a public institution done, that they should get it done in a first-class manner, and give first-class pay for it ...

Mr Gordon Smith, the Local Government Board architect...had referred to the pressing need of a hot water supply, which was wanted not only for the benefit of the inmates but for the interests of economy in the matter of fuel, which was considerable, increased tank accommodation, bathing arrangements, sanitary arrangements, and laundry fittings of a more adequate character. A pump-house had also been recommended. In the face of these resolutions leave to borrow a loan...had been obtained ... At the end of another year they were in this position—they had a great deal of money to spend, and had yet to make contracts for it ... When they were doing the work he thought they should take away the sheds against the sick wards, which were a great disadvantage ...

Now as to the matter of the drainage. When he inspected the house that week he brought down the medical inspector, Dr Fuller, with him, and, having thus the benefit of the experience and skill of a medical man, he was enabled to give the Board the results of those observations as well as of his own. On going to the boys' lavatory they at once noticed a very bad odour in the bathroom. He had the flooring taken up, and underneath was found an accumulation of six inches of water, with two inches of thick, black ooze. The stench was enough to sow the infection of diphtheria and zymotic disease all around. He at once ordered the deposit to be cleared away, and seven loads were taken out, the man who performed the work telling him that the stench was intolerable ...

He (Mr Bagenal) next dealt with the administration of the sick wards. He found that there were 169 inmates, of whom 59 were sick patients on the day he visited the house. This was a very large proportion, when it was remembered that the House was not full, and the people had not come in for the winter months. There were only two nurses ... He had no hesitation in saying that this was too great a burden to lay upon two people. A recent order which they had received from the Local Government Board would show them that the proper nursing of the sick was one of the questions which the Board laid the greatest possible stress upon ... The Medical Officer also was not satisfied with the general supervision of the sick, several cases he noticed not being attended to properly. Several of the beds were filled with the miscellaneous belongings of the inmates—all kinds of food, rags and sticks —and this consequent upon the nurses failing to sufficiently supervise the details of nursing ...

(continued overleaf)

The sheets on many of the beds were in a very bad state. This, however, he understood was being remedied. He had also been given to understand that the Board had supplied no pocket-handkerchiefs to the inmates, neither young nor old. If they sent children out to service he considered they should be sent out with the rudimentary elements of civilisation.

The Rev J BLAKE-HUMFREY—We always supply them with pocket-handkerchiefs.

The Rev H COLLISON—But what's the use of that if they don't know how to use them?

Mr BAGENAL said he was pleased to see them taking a step in advance. Dealing with the water supply, he said the bathing accommodation was deficient. He hoped that when they set up their boiler, about which they had been talking a year, they would be able to obtain a proper supply of hot water ...

Again, as regarded the dietary. The Board had had a great deal of trouble about the feeding of their people. He did not understand under what dietary scale they had been fed.

80. *Workhouse Administration at Gressenhall: Condemnatory Speech by Her Majesty's Inspector* (*Dereham and Fakenham Times*, 25 September 1897 [abridged]) This source, which provides useful insights into both the state of the workhouse and the attitudes of the guardians, illustrates the value of newspaper reports of guardians' meetings in comparison with the minute books. The minutes of the meeting on 20 September 1897 state merely that: 'Mr Bagenal H.M. Poor Law Inspector addressed the Guardians on various matters connected with the Workhouse', and that a vote of thanks was given.

COMPLAINT BY A PAUPER

An able bodied young man, an inmate in the House, came before the Board and said he wished to report the porter for knocking him about. The porter, he alleged, turned him out of the hall and then knocked him about with the keys, just because he spoke about the gruel, which was not fit to eat and "all full of blacks". The porter told him to hold his tongue, but he would not, and he was then turned out.

In reply to Mr WILSON, the young fellow said he was 27 years of age, and was a labourer from Litcham.

Mr WILSON—Don't you feel ashamed of yourself. I should think anything is good enough for you. I should like to give you a good sticking.

The inmate—I ain't lazy.

Mr HUDSON—You have heard the porter has been before the House committee?

The complainant replied that he had.

The CHAIRMAN—I quite agree with what has been said. It is a disgrace for you to be an inmate of the House at your age and with your strength. You ought to be earning your own living.

The inmate—I will go outside if you will find me work.

The CHAIRMAN—You can take your discharge when you like. If you had behaved yourself I am sure that the porter would not have interfered with you. As long as you are here you must behave yourself, and if you don't you can take yourself out. We don't want you here.

Complainant then left the room smiling.

81. *Complaint by a Pauper* (*Dereham and Fakenham Times*, 10 April 1897) This incident was not recorded in the minutes of the meeting on 5 April 1897—another illustration of the deficiency of the minute books as a source.

Individuals in the workhouse: a case study

This case study is an extension of the previous theme of life in the union workhouse. Reference has already been made to the possibility of reconstructing elements of the life histories of individual workhouse inmates or the careers of workhouse officers. Sometimes the sources allow the reconstruction of specific incidents in considerable detail, bringing the conditions of life in the workhouse, and contemporary attitudes, into sharp focus.

On 20 April 1868 Elizabeth Rudd, an inmate of Gressenhall Workhouse, gave birth to an illegitimate child. She was over 40 years old, and stated that the workhouse schoolmaster, Robert Bradfield, was the father of her child.

It is not known when Elizabeth Rudd was admitted to Gressenhall Workhouse, but she had certainly been an inmate for some years. She appears in the 1861 census enumerator's book for the workhouse (see source 82), together with her four illegitimate children. As an unmarried mother (or 'jacketer', as they were sometimes known at Gressenhall) Elizabeth would have suffered a discriminatory regime in the workhouse (see Source 63).

Robert Bradfield had been the workhouse schoolmaster at Gressenhall since 1840. Like all the officers, he lived on the site: he occupied a bedroom and a sitting room near the boys' dormitory. The schoolmaster's duties related exclusively to the workhouse boys. There was a separate school for the girls, under a schoolmistress, and for a time there was also a mixed school for the infants, under an infant schoolmistress. The schoolmaster was responsible not only for the boys' education but also for their health, welfare and demeanour. His life was isolated and constrained (see Sources 57 and 58).

The controversy with which this case study is concerned began on the morning of Monday 30 December 1867, when news of Elizabeth Rudd's pregnancy and her allegation concerning Robert Bradfield was brought to the attention of the board of guardians at its regular weekly meeting. Robert Bradfield denied any involvement with Elizabeth Rudd, and the guardians gave little credence to her story, 'owing mainly to the fact that she has heretofore given birth to four other illegitimate children', as the clerk explained in a letter to the poor law inspector, Sir John Walsham.

After the birth of the baby, Elizabeth Rudd continued to maintain that Robert Bradfield was the father, but declined to apply to a magistrate for the order of affiliation which would have made the father responsible for maintaining the child. In these circumstances, the guardians decided that there should be an official enquiry into the case. This was conducted at Gressenhall in July 1868 by Lieutenant Colonel P.B. Ward, who had taken over from Sir John Walsham as poor law inspector.

After the charge against Robert Bradfield had been found 'not proved', no further action was taken. Robert Bradfield carried on working at Gressenhall. When he retired in the summer of 1874, the guardians' testimonial stated that 'his general character and conduct has been unimpeachable'.

The sources for this case study are quite lengthy, but the compelling human detail means that they may prove more accessible to students than they appear at first sight.

Students might be asked to:

* consider the motivation of both Elizabeth Rudd and Robert Bradfield (assuming either that Robert Bradfield was the father of the child, or that he was not)

* reflect on the insights which the case study provides into daily life and attitudes in the workhouse

RETURN of all the PERSONS who SLEPT or ABODE in this INSTITUTION on the NIGHT of SUNDAY, APRIL 7th, 1861

NAME and SURNAME or Initials of Inmates in the Institution	(1) RELATION to Head of Family—or (2) Position	CONDITION	AGE (last birthday) of MALES	FEMALES	RANK, PROFESSION, or OCCUPATION	WHERE BORN	If Deaf-and-Dumb or Blind
Robert William Scraggs	Master	Married	46		Master of a Workhouse	Thetford, Suffolk	
Mary Ann Scraggs	Matron, wife of Master	"		49	Matron of the Workhouse	Croxton, Norfolk	
Thomas Butcher	Porter	"		58	Porter of a Workhouse	Shipdham, "	
Mary Anne Butcher	Assistant Matron, wife of the Porter	"		43	Assist. Matron of a Workhouse	Massingham, "	
Mary Anson	Nurse	Widow		66	Nurse in a Workhouse	Shipdham, "	
Robert Bradfield	Schoolmaster	Unmarried	42		Schoolmaster in a Workhouse	Bintry, "	
Sarah Ormiston	Schoolmistress	"		24	Schoolmistress in a Workhouse	Lynn, "	
Green Anna	Infant Schoolmistress	"		20	Infant Schoolmistress in a Workhouse	Gressenhall,"	
Rudd Elizabeth	Pauper	"		33	Almswoman late Domestic servt	Elmham, Norfolk	
Rudd Eve	"	"		17	Almswoman late Domestic servt	Elmham, Norfolk	
Rudd Susanna	"	"		12	Scholar	Gressenhall, Norfolk	
Rudd Sarah Ann	"	"		8			
Rudd Walter	"	"		5			
Graves Mary Ann	"	Unmarried		31	Almswoman late Dressmaker	Gressenhall, Norfolk	
Graves Ann	"	"		8	Scholar	Gressenhall, "	

82. *Extracts from the Census Enumerator's Book for Gressenhall Workhouse, 7 April 1861* (Public Record Office, RG9 1242) At Gressenhall, successive masters chose not to preserve the anonymity of the workhouse inmates: the names therefore appear in full in each census.

Mitford and Launditch Union

Statement of *Elizabeth Rudd* a pauper Inmate of the Workhouse at Gressenhall.
This Examinant Saith as follows:—

I have been in the house 12 years the 11th of last October. I am 43 years of age or thereabouts and have never been married. I have now four Bastard children living. The eldest is about 24 years of age and the youngest is upwards of 12. They are not all by one man. For the last 9 or 10 years I have been employed to clean up the boys bedroom—and the room used as a bed room and sitting room by Mr Bradfield, the Schoolmaster. For some time past he has from time to time occasionally made me small presents, by way of acknowledgement for doing up his room, and sometimes he has caught hold of my dress as I passed him, but he never took any liberty with me until one Sunday in the month of June last, when he sent the little boy 'Eke' for me about a Prayer Book which Mr Bradfield could not find. I went to his room in consequence about 1/2 past 9 or 10 with the Boy Eke and when I went in he came out and went away. As soon as I got in I said to Mr Bradfield "How is it that your book is misplaced I hav'nt seen it anywhere" and he said, laughing "I dont want the Book I want you" and he put his arms round my waist I said "What are you after", and he expressed what his feelings were to me and said he had thought about it a score of times but he never dare attempt it before. He then pulled up my clothes and had connexion with me. He did not then give me any money. The next time he had similar intercourse with me was on a Thursday in the month of July between 2 and 3 o'clock in the afternoon when I went up to do his room. The third time was in the latter part of July also on a Thursday when I went up to do his room as before. I found myself in the family way in July and I expect to be confined in the latter part of next March or the beginning of April. I told Mr Bradfield in the month of August that I was in the family way. He made no other reply then than "I hope that is not the case, I think you must be mistaken, there cannot be anything the matter with you". About a fortnight afterwards I was doing up his room as usual, when he said to me, "How do you get on". I replied "It is as I told you" and he said "Can't you go out for a week" I said "No, I have no where to go to" and he said—"Can't you get leave for a day and go to some midwife to do something for you" I said "I don't know where to go for such a thing as that I never took anything in my life". He then laid me 5/- down on the table and said "if you won't take it for anything else, take it for cleaning the room". I refused to take the 5/- and took one only. He then promised to see me again in a few weeks and wished me to make up my mind and see if I could not do anything myself. He saw me again in October and asked me to go out of the house and he offered me £5 to go to Norwich saying it would be his ruin if I said the child was his. I told him I could not say it was any other persons for I would take my oath that since I had my last child I had never known any other man but him. He asked me how long I could keep it a secret and I told him I could not keep it unknown longer than Christmas, and he said "If you don't say it is mine I'll befriend you, I don't care about staying here longer than March and then I shall go to my Sisters in London. She keeps a large Inn and I will think of you." On the Monday before Xmas day he came to me and said "I should have come to you on my room and had some talk with you but I thought I was watched". He again begged of me not to say it was his and told me that I might say the Father of the child was not here. I have not been out of the house for a night during the last year except last June, when, by permission of the Board I went out for two days and a night. I went on that occasion to see my daughter (Elizabeth Spooner) at Bintry and I went out with the woman Graves who can speak to my conduct while I was out, and so can both my daughters". I am ready to swear that Mr Bradfield and no other person is the father of the child I am pregnant with and if he is put on his oath he could not deny it.

     her
Elizabeth X Rudd
     mark

Thomas Eke aged 11 an Inmate of the Workhouse, says I recollect being sent one Sunday by Mr Bradfield to Elizabeth Rudd about his prayer book which was missing. I went to her and she came back with me and went upstairs into Mr Bradfield's room. I did not see her go into the room but, she went up the stairs and I remained below in the yard. This was about 10 o'clock in the morning I did not see her come down again. This was sometime last summer, before I went up to the sick room. It never happened but once that I know of.
Thomas Eke

83. ***Statement of Elizabeth Rudd, a Pauper Inmate of the workhouse at Gressenhall, 13 January 1868*** (Public Record Office, MH12 8483)

Proceedings of an Enquiry held at the Mitford and Launditch Union Workhouse on 20th July 1868
Elizabeth Rudd an inmate of the Workhouse for the last 12 years being duly sworn states:—[the first part of her statement was similar to her earlier one, reproduced as Source 72] in November last I was sleeping with another woman, Mary Anne Graves, I had slept with her several years. She told me she thought there was something the matter with me. I said, yes, there was. She asked me who was the father of the child. I said nothing. She then pressed me to say, and she said she believed it was Mr Bradfield, as she never knew that I was with any one else. I did not deny it. I heard nothing more until December, the Monday before Christmas, when I was called in by the Governor and Matron and they accused me of being in the family way as it was reported about the house that I was so by an Officer in the house. I said yes it was so. The Matron said was it by Mr Bradfield. I said yes it was. I then was taken before the Visiting Committee and answered in the same way. Upon several occasions I was brought before the Board of Guardians and Visiting Committee and I always adhered to the same story. Mr Bradfield was present upon one occasion. After I had reported the case to the Matron another woman was appointed to clean out his room in my place. I was confined on the 20th April, 1868—and I still adhere to my statement on oath that the child is Mr Bradfield's and no other person's ...
Qn. by Inspector to Elizabeth Rudd. When was the last time that you were out of the house and for how long?
A. About the beginning of June, and I was out two days and one night. I went to see my daughters one married at Bintry to a labourer, the other in service with Mr Lede a farmer at Guist. In July I went to Mr Norton's at Hoe, and took my little girl to service there. It was in the afternoon and I returned by tea-time. I have several times been to see my girl at Mr Norton's for an hour or two since-but I have never slept out of the house since june.
Qn. by Inspector. Did you go out by yourself when you slept out in June?
A. I went out with Mary Ann Graves. She was with me the whole time with the exception of an hour or two when I went to see my daughter in service. Mary Ann Graves also slept with me on the night I was out.
(continued overleaf)

Mary Ann Graves being duly sworn states I am an inmate of Gressenhall Workhouse where I have been for the last two years and a half. I know Elizabeth Rudd. She was an inmate of the house when I came in. I slept in the same bed with her. She had to do out Mr Bradfield's room. On the 3rd June 1867, I asked permission to go out with Elizabeth Rudd. On the 5th I went out with her and we returned together on the 6th. I was with her the whole time. She went to her daughter's. We slept at her daughter's at Bintry. We both slept in the same bed. On the morning of the 6th Elizabeth Rudd went to see her daughter in service for an hour or so. We returned together to the workhouse in the evening. I think it was after the bell had rung. In November last I accused Elizabeth Rudd of being in the family way. She said yes she was. I said whoever is it by? and she began to cry. I said it must be by Mr Bradfield as she had been nowhere else—and she said it was.

Qn. by Mr Bradfield. Had Elizabeth Rudd any opportunity of speaking to other men? A. Not to my knowledge. She was employed in looking after the boys' room, and on Thursday afternoon Mr Bradfield's.

Thomas Eke being duly sworn states I have been an inmate of the Workhouse about 4 years. I am 12 years old. One Sunday morning about a year ago in the summer time Mr Bradfield sent me to Betsy Rudd in the jacketers' yard to ask her for a prayer-book. She went upstairs to see him about it. I went back to the School.

Robert William Scraggs late Master of the Workhouse being duly sworn states Elizabeth Rudd came to me on the 30th December 1867, and in the presence of the Matron declared herself to be in the family way which I immediately reported to the Visiting Committee and entered in the book. She said she was pregnant by the Schoolmaster, Mr Bradfield. She was employed by the Matron to look after the boys' rooms and also the Schoolmaster's. She had been selected for this duty as a most respectable hard-working woman, and although I am aware that she had had four bastard children before coming to the house, her conduct in the house was always most praiseworthy and respectable. I know that Elizabeth Rudd had leave for one night in the summer of last year and upon several occasions she used to go out for an hour or so to wash the clothes of her daughter in service, by permission of the Matron.

Qn. by Mr Bradfield. Did you ever see me take the slightest liberty with any woman in the house; or in any way behave improperly to them; or had you any reason to believe that I did so.

A. Never.

Robert Bradfield Schoolmaster being duly sworn states I have been twenty-eight years and four months Schoolmaster in the Gressenhall Workhouse. I have only to say that I utterly deny ever having had any connection with Elizabeth Rudd and that I am not the father of the child she has given birth to. I never took any liberties with her.

P. B. Ward
Lt. Colonel
Inspector of Poor Law

84. *Proceedings of an Enquiry held at the Mitford and Launditch Union Workhouse, 20 July 1868* (Public Record Office, MH12 8483)

Rougham
Bury St Edmunds
28th July 1868

My Lords and Gentlemen,
Agreeably to the instructions contained in your letter dated 13th July 1868 ... I proceeded to Gressenhall workhouse and met the Board of Guardians of the *Mitford and Launditch Union* on the 20th July 1868—and I then held an official enquiry into the charge preferred by Elizabeth Rudd against Mr Bradfield, the Schoolmaster at the workhouse. I annex a copy of the evidence as given before me on oath.

In recording my opinion that the charge is *not proved* against Mr Bradfield, I feel it my duty to draw the attention of the Board to the *persistently consistent* manner in which Elizabeth Rudd has throughout adhered to her statements, and to the absence of any evidence of her ever having had an opportunity for intercourse with any other man in the workhouse. The occasion of Elizabeth Rudd's absence from the workhouse, which it was sought to fasten upon her as that when she had become pregnant by some person outside the workhouse, is shown to have occurred on the night of 6th June 1867, *ten months and a half* before the child was born, viz 20th April 1868. This at once disposes of such a charge, and moreover every hour of that absence appears to me to be most satisfactorily accounted for.

It is a well-established fact that the difficulties of *proof* in such a case as the present are almost insuperable. No doubt Mr Bradfield had many opportunities of committing the crime without a chance of its being witnessed, and Elizabeth Rudd's statement is clear in every detail. On the other hand such a charge might be trumped up against a perfectly innocent man who could bring no evidence to refute it. Moreover, on the one hand Mr Bradfield has been 28 years and 4 months schoolmaster at the workhouse, and has throughout borne an unimpeachable character, whereas, unfortunately for her, Elizabeth Rudd's early career does not bear investigation, she having given birth to five illegitimate children previous to the present one, although the youngest of them is nearly 13 years of age. On the one side or on the other no doubt deliberate perjury has been committed, but I feel bound to say, after mature consideration, that in my opinion Elizabeth Rudd has failed to *prove* the charge she preferred against Mr Bradfield.

I have the Honor to be
My Lords and Gentlemen
Your obed[ien]t Humble Servant
P B Ward L[ieutenan]t Colonel
Inspector of Poor Law

To the Honourable
The Poor Law Board
[additional note, in different handwriting]
The President
I agree with Col. Ward
It seems most improbable that Mr Bradfield, after an apparently irreproachable service of 28 years, should have committed the offence with which he is charged—especially as Elizabeth Rudd had been for the last 13 years in the habit of cleaning out his room, and he is not charged with having attempted anything of the kind until now. The evidence of a woman who has had 5 bastards before, needs, to my mind, *very strong* confirmation before it can be believed.

85. *Letter concerning the enquiry into the case of Rudd and Bradfield*: from Lt. Col. P.B. Ward, poor law inspector, to the Poor Law Board, 28 July 1868 (Public Record Office, MH12 8483)

BIBLIOGRAPHY

1. Recent General Works

Anstruther, I., *The Scandal of the Andover Workhouse* (1984)

Boyer, G.R., *An Economic History of the English Poor Law 1750-1850* (1990)

Brundage, A., *The Making of the New Poor Law* (1978)

Crowther, M.A., *The Workhouse System* (1981)

Digby, A., *Pauper Palaces* (1978)

Digby, A., *The Poor Law in Nineteenth Century England and Wales* (1982)

Driver, F., *Power and Pauperism: The Workhouse System, 1834-84* (1993)

Edsall, N.C., *The Anti-Poor Law Movement 1834-44* (1971)

Fraser, D. (ed.), *The New Poor Law in the Nineteenth Century* (1976)

Gibson, J., et al., *Poor Law Union Records* [published by the Federation of Family History Societies, 1993]: pt.1 South east England and East Anglia; pt.2 The Midlands and Northern England; pt.3 South West England, the Marches and Wales; pt.4 Gazetteer of England and Wales

Johnstone, V.J., *Diet in Workhouses and Prisons, 1835-1895* (1985)

Knott, J., *Popular Opposition to the 1834 Poor Law* (1986)

Longmate, N., *The Workhouse* (1974)

Rose, M.E., *The English Poor Law 1780-1930* (1971)

Rose, M.E., *The Relief of Poverty 1834-1914* (1972)

Rose, M.E. (ed.), *The Poor and the City: the English Poor Law in its Urban Context 1834-1914* (1985)

Snell, K.D.M., *Annals of the Labouring Poor* (1985)

Thane, P., 'Women and the Poor Law in Victorian England', *History Workshop Journal*, 6 (1978)

Treble, J.H., *Urban Poverty in Britain 1830-1914* (1983)

Williams, K., *From Pauperism to Poverty* (1981)

Wood, P., *Poverty and the Workhouse in Victorian Britain* (1991)

2. Local Studies

This is not an exhaustive list, and new local studies appear regularly. It is also well worthwhile to check the transactions or journals of local and county history societies, as these frequently include articles concerning the poor law and its operation.

(continued ...)

Bilyard, J., *Hales Hospital: from workhouse to hospital* (1987) [Heckingham Workhouse, Norfolk]

Caplan, M., *In the Shadow of the Workhouse* (1984) [the new poor law in Nottinghamshire, 1836-1846]

Cole, J., *Down Poorhouse Lane: the Diary of a Rochdale Workhouse* (1984)

Coleman, N.C., *People, Poverty and Protest in Hoxne Hundred 1780-1880* (1982) [Suffolk]

Crowley, J. and Reid, A.W., *The Poor Law in Norfolk, 1700-1850* (1983)

Dorset County Council, *Dorset Workhouses* (1980)

Fowler, S., *Philanthropy and the Poor Law in Richmond, 1836-71* (1991) [Surrey]

Hayward, N. and Windridge, N., *Badges and Beans: the annals of the poor of Yetminster Hundred* (1989) [Dorset]

Land, N., *Victorian Workhouse: a study of the Bromsgrove Union Workhouse, 1836-1901* (1990) [Worcestershire]

Langley, M. and G., *At the Crossroads: a history of Arclid Workhouse and Hospital* (1993) [Cheshire]

Murphy, M.J., *Poverty in Cambridgeshire* (1978)

Reid, A.W., *Fire at the Workhouse: a study in cause and motive* (1988) [Heckingham Workhouse, Norfolk]

Robbins, A., *The workhouse at Purton and the Cricklade and Wootton Basset Union* (1992) [Wiltshire]

School of Humanities, Humberside College of Education, *The New Poor Law in Humberside* (1986)

Surtees, J., *Barracks, Workhouse and Hospital: the story of St. Mary's, Eastbourne, 1794-1990* (1992)

Westbourne Local History Group, *The Westbourne Union: life in and out of the new workhouse* (1991) [West Sussex]

White, G., et al., *In and Out of the Workhouse: the coming of the new poor law to Cambridgeshire and Huntingdonshire* (1978)

3. Books for Schools

Styles, S.J., *The Poor Law* (Macmillan 'History in Depth' series, 1987)

Taylor, D., *Poverty* (Heinemann History series, 1988)

Watson, R., *Edwin Chadwick, Poor Law and Public Health* (Longman 'Then and There' series, 1969) [still useful]

Wood, T., *Playback: History Roleplays* (Edward Arnold, 1982) [includes a roleplay set in 'Westford Workhouse']

INDEX

References to Gressenhall Workhouse and Mitford and Launditch Union are very numerous throughout the book and have not been indexed.

NOTES